THE COMPLETE BOOK OF ARTISTS' TECHNIQUES

Kurt Herberts

THE COMPLETE BOOK OF

ARTISTS' TECHNIQUES

80 COLOR PLATES
89 MONOCHROME ILLUSTRATIONS
28 DRAWINGS

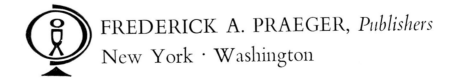

FREDERICK A. PRAEGER, *Publishers*
New York · Washington

TRANSLATED FROM THE GERMAN 'DIE MALTECHNIKEN'
PUBLISHED BY ECON-VERLAG DÜSSELDORF

BOOKS THAT MATTER

Published in the United States of America in 1958
by Frederick A. Praeger, Inc., Publishers
111 Fourth Avenue, New York, N.Y. 10003
Second printing, 1960
Third printing, 1963
Fourth printing, 1965
Fifth printing, 1969
All rights reserved
© 1950 by Thames & Hudson
Library of Congress Catalog Card Number: 58-12424
Printed in Great Britain

The understanding of artists' techniques gives rise to a complex of questions which have occupied me for many years. In conjunction with a number of distinguished artists and technicians, I have also made numerous practical experiments connected with the development, particular resources, expressive power, and limitations of different techniques. The theme of the present book emerged in the course of these experiments; therefore, this is not as first may appear, a purely theoretical work, but is based on practical foundations laid over a long period.

Some of the material which I have used in my previous works—which have not been available in the English language—has been added as an appendix to this book, enhancing its value and rounding off the subject.

I should like to express my thanks to the artists, Willi Baumeister, Georg Muche and Oskar Schlemmer; to the museum directors and experts—and especially to Professor Ferdinand Lammeyer—who gave me their very kind co-operation and supplied me with specialist information, without which it would have been impossible to write this book; also to my scientific assistant, Dr Beatrix v. Ragué, who gave me her support throughout its preparation.

Wuppertal, Spring, 1958   *Kurt Herberts*

CONTENTS

I

THE NATURE

IMPORTANCE AND INVESTIGATION

OF ARTISTS' TECHNIQUES

It is a curious fact that the average layman is so ignorant of the technical aspect of painting that it does not occur to him that the subject might be worth investigation. Reproductions in books, calendars, postcards, and even films are the means whereby we usually become acquainted with works of art in the first place, but they obviously provide us with only very superficial knowledge. Anyone who has looked at a painting by van Gogh knows that its character depends largely on the impasto consisting of little ridges and valleys of solid paint made by the strokes of a heavily loaded brush, i.e. on the quality of the paint itself, and he remembers that he reads the artist's handwriting by following the course of these brush strokes. Neither this nor countless other indications of the power of technique can be transmitted by photography or colour reproduction. When this picture is reproduced on glossy art paper it becomes flattened out and scarcely looks different from a reproduction of a painting executed, say, in encaustic or tempera, although in fact the originals could hardly differ more, either from each other or from the reproduction. It is true that the enormous gap between original and reproduction is becoming smaller through the great improvement in the quality of colour reproductions, but the discrepancy is still present; therefore, to appreciate fully the significance of technique and how much it contributes to the conveying of intellectual force, we must look at the original. It is therefore worth while making a comprehensive study of these techniques. We must consider them as more than mere handicrafts; we must inquire into their very essence.

Even the layman can see that the individual techniques vary from each other in temperament and character. Let us, for instance, imagine a picture of a sunrise, in which the delicate mother-of-pearl tints of the sky merge into one another softly; this picture could very conceivably be painted in watercolours, but it can hardly be imagined as a mosaic. Equally impossible would it be to convey the dryness and brittleness of an Expressionist woodcut with a silverpoint drawing. Any number of such examples can be quoted, but they all illustrate the fact that the differences between the techniques are so fundamental that one cannot be confused with another.

Now, to find out what these differences are we must examine each technique in turn, though a cursory glance is enough to show us their main characteristics. For instance, we can clearly see that some techniques are intimate in character and are used to best advantage on a small scale, while others require broader treatment; similarly, that some make use of transparent colours and others of opaque ones; that some tend to blur the outlines of forms and others show them in clear contrast. And it is also obvious that some techniques work in a linear way while others depend on colour and tone. It is the *quality* of oil paint that differs from that of watercolour, and the quality of a drawing in red chalk from that of a woodcut —in the same way as in an orchestra, the flute, the horn, the violin, and the harpsichord sound quite different even if they are playing the same tune. The first and fundamental thing, therefore, which we must thoroughly understand about techniques, is that the differences between them are basic; they are not interchangeable. Of course we may ask whether it matters in which technique the artist chooses to express himself provided he really has something to say. Indeed, the particular thing the artist wishes to say can only be said in *one* particular way; in other words, each artistic conception can only have one ideal technical realization. The progress from the artist's original idea to the completed picture is a transformation of spirit into matter. In the painted picture these two elements cease to be distinguishable; they unite and thenceforth speak the same language. The artist, exercising complete mastery over the media, has revealed their potentialities and finally, through his creative power, has overcome the material itself. The essential result of this process is an image that reflects the spirit of the artist and is communicated to us through forms and colours on a flat plane.

Although the actual materials that go into the making of a picture—such as wood, canvas, stonework, oil paint, tempera or crayon—are not in themselves of its essence, they contribute to it. Both they and the technique are agents with whose help the idea in the artist's mind is transformed into a visible work of art, but they are not neutral in the sense of being mutually interchangeable. The distinctions between one and another can be compared to the differences between the organs of the body; like these, each performs a quite specific function. For in each painting technique is latent an individual potentiality, which, as a contributory force, is brought to life by the artist in his work. He may use this potentiality in the right or in the wrong way; but it is there, and it is subject to laws of its own, so that he cannot ignore it.

Erich Schwebsch, whose writings on aesthetics are based on Rudolf Steiner's teaching, said that 'the artist, who knows and loves his medium so well, has not as much power over it as the pure "technician" who feels that he is master of nature. For he now encounters an experience which surreptitiously reveals itself to him, the "veneration for that which is beneath him". And we may say with conviction that the genuine artist now discovers that the seemingly dead material actually has its own "freedom"—if the word is not misunderstood —its own essence, which he must respect if he is to transform it into a likeness of life, if *it* is to speak the language of art. . . . The artist therefore finally encounters a moral element in his technique, and he speaks with good reason of truth and falsehood in this very field. It is just this which we should marvel at, namely that the artist, who would never dream of judging his art on the "spiritual" plane or look for any external, moral motive, should discover, just at the moment when he is becoming absorbed, as he thinks, in the amoral sphere of technique, the inner relevance of a moral nuance without which technique becomes for him something downright sub-human.'

The sculptor Karl Knappe once expressed the problem in these words: 'The crisis through which art is passing is one that concerns not the essence of art itself but the artistic media. An image cannot be created without regard for the laws of nature, and each kind of material has natural laws of its own. Every block of stone, every piece of wood is subject to its own rules. Every medium has, so to speak, its own tempo: the tempo of a pencil or a piece of charcoal is quite different from the tempo of a woodcut. But the habit of mind which creates, for instance, a pen drawing cannot simply be applied mechanically to the making of a woodcut; to do this would be to deny the validity of the spiritual, as well as the technical tempo.'

We may compare the various painting techniques with the various languages. The language of a people reflects its particular experience of the world as any other national characteristic does, and if we regard it merely as a means of communication we overlook its deeper, artistic possibilities. Every language has words which are untranslatable, whose shade of meaning is unique and cannot be reproduced exactly in another language even by the closest synonym. In other words, some languages have expressions for certain nuances of feeling or experience which others do not. And with the techniques of painting it is the same; the character, the expressive power, the 'language' of one are untranslatable into those of another.

What, then, is the artist's position with regard to these facts? In the first place we must be aware that he also has his own spiritual and technical tempo; the creation of every work of art is therefore a process of multiple analysis and penetration, ending in the utmost degree of correspondence between his original conception and the final form of the picture.[1]

The artist knows the differences between one technique's expressive power and that of

16

another and chooses the one most suitable to his temperament, at the same time remembering that all techniques have limitations which must not be overstepped. In his attempt to find the final form a picture shall take he often also tries new ways of eliminating the obstacles presented by the technique, and endeavours to develop a method which will exactly communicate his idea. To do this he must 'subordinate his will to the laws governing the material'; at the same time 'the forces inherent in the material . . . will incorporate the artist's will in their final expression, yielding on the one hand the work of art, and on the other, knowledge of the laws by which the material is governed. These laws reveal themselves to the artist's mind while he is working.'[2] 'Through his technique, which is guided by prophetic imagination tutored in accurate sense-perception, the artist becomes the demonstrator of hidden laws which without him would have scarcely been revealed.'[3]

Sometimes the artist wishes to say something which the technique he has chosen is incapable of expressing, with the result that his pictures may look 'tormented', a pitfall with which all artists are familiar. But if he avails himself of all the innate resources of the technique and uses them correctly, then is revealed that 'rare and magic power of the material brought to life'[4] which is one of the inexhaustible wonders of a great work of art. No technique offers boundless possibilities, but 'new forms grow out of the very limitations of the medium; they stimulate the artist to fresh creative activity and form his style. Progress in art consists not in widening its boundaries, but in seeing them more clearly.'[5]

Although a few artists like Dürer and Menzel created equally great masterpieces concurrently in two very different techniques, it is much more common for an artist to restrict himself almost entirely to a single technique, once he has found the one which is most congenial to him. Not only individuals but even whole periods have their predilections, and from these we may draw certain conclusions about the aims which preoccupied them.

For instance, in the age of exploration and discovery when artists aspired to represent the outward appearance of things in the greatest and most accurate detail possible, the prevalent drawing medium was silverpoint. But in the High Renaissance the emphasis shifted; this period was interested, not in accurate description but in the plastic quality of form, which is illustrated by the increasing use of red chalk instead of silverpoint. Pastel took the place of red chalk in the Rococo period, most likely because that age loved the 'beauty of nature', which was reflected in another way by the popularity of pastoral plays. This kind of analogy should not be stretched too far, but there is no doubt that changes of medium have some bearing on changes in style.

Strangely enough, a systematic study of painting techniques in which their individual qualities are considered has scarcely ever been attempted. Textbooks on single techniques are content to deal mainly with the practical aspects; a mere craftsman's acquaintance with materials is however not sufficient.[6] On the other hand, books concerned with specifically artistic problems hardly ever go beyond the consideration of form, style, and intellectual development to question the nature of technique.

The first attempt to raise this question appears to have been made by the artists of the Bauhaus (it would, incidentally, be well worth while to follow up its development). At all events, from the nineteen-twenties onwards we find occasional references to the question of the distinctive properties of techniques; the reason is possibly to be found in the new developments which were then taking place in architecture, for which entirely new vistas were opened up by steel and reinforced concrete construction, and as a result the formal and expressive values of different techniques came under discussion.

In 1934, Henri Focillon's book *La Vie des Formes* was published. 'It is tempting to believe,' Focillon says, 'that certain techniques might be practised equally well in any medium. Take drawing, for instance, in which the medium is subjected to such a strict process of abstraction that it is reduced to the status of an insignificant accessory, and in fact is almost sublimated. Yet it is still matter, even in this volatile state; in fact, it acquires an unusual power through this very process of being exploited, in which it is here concentrated and there diffused. Considering the great variety of drawing media, to mention only ink, wash, pencil, black chalk, red chalk and crayon, and considering that each of these can be used either alone or with one of the others, it is evident that there must be as great a variety of modes and qualities of expression. In order to convince ourselves entirely, let us for a moment imagine the impossible, namely a red chalk drawing by Watteau copied by Ingres in pencil, or, simpler still . . . a charcoal drawing copied in wash. This copy has acquired quite unexpected qualities; it is in fact an entirely new work of art. It is well known what happens when an oil painting is reproduced in mosaic or tapestry. On the other hand, the master engravers who reproduced oil paintings were well aware that their task was to rival the paintings no more than the painter had attempted to rival nature, but to transpose them into a different medium. We might enlarge on this with profit, since it helps us to understand that every work of art is unique.'

Although Focillon has raised some vital questions about techniques in this and the following passages of his book, and has indeed made some important assertions about them, he has only devoted a single chapter—albeit a very important one—to this problem. He has pointed the way, but he has not followed up his own ideas, and above all, he has not studied the individual techniques in detail. In our view, however, a detailed inquiry of this kind is essential.

The closest approach to such an inquiry is Ferdinand Lammeyer's book, *Maltechnik für Kunstfreunde*, published in 1949. O. v. Pander also touches on important relevant problems in his publication *Vom Wesen und Werden des Kunstwerks*, and Max Burchartz refers to them in his *Gestaltungslehre*. Burchartz, however, restricts his investigation of 'the psychophysical powers of expression latent in the material potentialities of medium' mainly to individual colours, forms, and space relationships, and in so doing he is following the same track as those numerous artists who have written about art. They too emphasize how important it is that the artist should fully understand his medium, but for them the word 'medium' has a different meaning; it implies, in fact, the resources not of the technique but of the colours and forms—the plane, the circle, line, brightness, tonality, interrelations, balance of tensions, and so forth.

More recently there has been a conspicuous tendency for occasional references to technical details to appear in museum catalogues. This trend could on the face of it be accounted for by the current interest in technology, but a more valid reason is probably that the author, at least, has recognized the distinct artistic language of the technique he is discussing. But we have yet to discover a coherent study of all, or at least of most of the techniques used in painting, with emphasis on their individual properties and resources.

Gottfried Semper defined a work of art as in the main the result of the medium and the technical procedure.[7] Far be it from us to resume this purely technical approach, for it shifts the emphasis from the eminently intellectual character of artistic creation to a physical process. Nevertheless, there is some truth in what Semper says. A work of art does not exist *per se*; it exists only in the one particular form which it has been given by the artist— by virtue of technique. As we have shown, the difference between the techniques does not lie in what the *artist* can do with them, but in their own intrinsically different expressional properties. Even two pictures of a single object made by the same artist, one, let us say, in pastel and the other in oils, *must* look completely different, for the artist has used two different artistic organs, so to speak, to put a single conception into visible form; the results cannot, therefore, be identical.

In an analysis such as has been attempted in the second part of this book, that is, one in which the scope and limitations of each technique are singled out, it is very difficult to avoid bias or exaggeration. For a technique in itself does not automatically lead to certain results; it is the artist, the inspired man, who must arouse the latent, and partly dormant, qualities possessed by each technique and evaluate them correctly. Here, however, we can discuss only those qualities inherent in the techniques themselves, no more than hinting at, and leaving open, the ways in which the artist can make use of them. It is therefore self-evident that we cannot simply classify the techniques by means of clichés. What is more, the book will fail in its purpose if an isolated technique is singled out for reference, because its quality can only be appreciated in relation to another technique. For this is not a reference book; its point of departure is the question why each technique represents, in its role of mediating agent between an idea and its realization, a different way of realizing this idea; this question can only be answered by a general survey of the largest practicable number of techniques. It is not an encyclopedia made up of disconnected entries; rather it is like a drawing consisting of many lines which, seen together, form a picture of the diversity of ways in which the artist can express an idea. In this kind of closely knit treatment a strictly systematic arrangement is neither necessary nor possible. It is sufficient to group together those techniques which are interrelated.

Our inquiry is divided into three parts, under the heading of the three elements of which technique is made up: the support, the tools and the materials, whose interaction has already been discussed elsewhere.[8] Although each of these elements plays a part in every technique, there is always one which is more conspicuous than the others, and the technique usually takes its name from it. The first section consists of techniques in which the ground is the most important factor; for instance, stone, plaster, wood, ivory or glass. The second deals with those which are called after the medium, i.e. the pigments and their vehicles, such as pastel, watercolour, tempera and oil paint, wax paint or lacquer; the third, with those which are called after the implement (pen, brush, etc.).

There are one or more illustrations devoted to each technique, and although they too are naturally open to the criticism levelled at all process reproduction earlier on, because it is just the technical features which they conceal almost entirely, we have wherever possible used the most characteristic examples. In addition, several techniques have been analysed pictorially, so that they can be studied phase by phase.

Some techniques have inevitably been left out—there are too many isolated cases and there is too much overlapping, for every one to be mentioned. Nor must the reader expect to find an exhaustive treatment of all the processes which the practice of a technique involves; this kind of information will be found in works of reference, for which allowances have been made in the text. In the author's opinion it is of greater value to discover systematically what a technique can offer and what it cannot, wherein its own peculiar strength and uniqueness lies. We hope that our observations may contribute to an ever better understanding of great works of art.

II

ANALYSIS OF

INDIVIDUAL TECHNIQUES

1

TECHNIQUES MAINLY

DEPENDENT ON

THE SUPPORT OR GROUND

SUPPORT AND GROUND:	Primary rock, either in damp caves, or exposed (damp or dry)
MATERIALS:	Earth colours in their natural state (in lumps). Ochres of various colours. Black manganese earth. Iron oxides. Wood charcoal. Binding media (possibly; but no longer verifiable). If used, these may have included honey, milk, animal fats, and blood (*N.B.* Fat will hardly adhere to damp rock and blood blackens). Even if used, they cannot have played a decisive part in preserving the paintings, as in reconstruction of the technique the colours adhered well to the rock when dissolved only in water
TOOLS:	Probably included: primitive brushes made from birds' feathers and small sticks, pads of fur, the human hand, occasionally hollow cylindrical bones for spraying

The earliest artistic achievements of man were not studied scientifically until very recently, in fact not until the present century. It was only in 1901, when the cave paintings of Font-de-Gaume and les Combarelles were discovered, that it was acknowledged that these and the paintings of Altamira—which had been known for quite some time—were in fact creations of the Ice Age. In spite of the astronomical distance of time which separates us from this epoch[9] so many finds have now been made that we can venture some fairly positive statements about these paintings. The difficult problem of the purpose for which

Horses, ibex, and hands. Franco-Cantabrian cave painting

Group of warriors. Eastern Spanish rock painting

they were painted—whether in connection with hunting or other magic, or to what extent they are the results of a primitive impulse to paint—need not detain us here. We are chiefly concerned with the technique and its expressive possibilities.

In contrast to all later techniques, the ground on which these rock paintings were executed was not made artificially and then laid on a support: the living rock served as ground and support in one. The surface had to be accepted as it was, and the procedure used in painting on it was therefore very largely determined by the structural peculiarities and other properties of the rock. The painting ground was absorbent because the rock was porous; the tectonic structure of the rock surface, its roughness or smoothness, for instance, determined the way in which tools and materials had to be handled, and the more accentuated protuberances were directly utilized in the painting. The materials used were lumps of coloured earth sharpened into primitive crayons, or liquid colour painted directly on to the rock. Many of these sharpened fragments of coloured earth have now been found, and so have countless dishes in which the colours were ground and mixed.

As a consequence of these two techniques, the one a kind of pastel and the other *al prima* painting, the execution was monumental and sweeping, the composition was grand and the forms were simple. At Altamira, for instance, effects of great liveliness and naturalism were obtained by the exploitation of the irregular rock structure: form and perspective seem to have been completely mastered by these early artists. This direct method of painting, with its vigorous colour execution, was in complete harmony with the rough ground and support. It also answered a hunting community's desire for accuracy and naturalism, because it is most likely that these paintings were used in the practice of hunting magic and the more life-like the animals were, the better. We do not find such realistic and expressive paintings again until many thousands of years later, at the height of the Cretan civilization.

Between these cave paintings and the rock paintings found in eastern Spain, such as those in the Valltorta Gorge, thousands of years elapsed. These were executed under quite different conditions, on smooth rock faces, in fact, which allowed a more circumspect technique and so a more delicate rendering of form. On the other hand there were no irregularities in the rock there, like those in the caves of Franco-Cantabria, which could be used to accentuate the plasticity of the forms and give an illusion of space. The rock paintings of eastern Spain have a silhouette-like appearance and are mostly painted in monochrome. They are worked with brushes, in two layers, with a kind of glazing technique. As a consequence of this method the scale of the work was small, since one line represented one brushload of paint; the forms were flat and stylized.

These rock drawings are in fact the first evidence of a movement towards stylization which became gradually more pronounced and ended in abstraction.[10] Research has shown that this evolution of style was connected with a development in thought. The progress from hunting to agricultural communities may also have had something to do with it. The change was evident not only in style but in the technique, which altered to suit the new demands; this is how the vehement paintings of Franco-Cantabria, executed in flat body colour, were replaced by the thinly glazed rock paintings of eastern Spain.

SUPPORT AND GROUND:	Masonry, covered with sand and lime mortar in layers, the surface layer containing marble-dust. This covered with coat of tinted plaster, which is the painting surface. The painting is smoothed with a hot iron
MATERIALS:	Pigments which resist lime. Glass frits for green and blue colour. Admixtures of organic substances. Bland soap
TOOLS:	Plasterers' tools for application of ground. Round brushes for painting. Iron with bevelled edges, for ironing finished work

The paintings found at Pompeii and Herculaneum have excited a great deal of attention ever since these two towns, which were buried by an eruption of Vesuvius, were rediscovered and excavated. Archaeologists, artists, and experts on art were all fascinated by the highly developed technique in which these works must have been executed, characterized by the gently reflective sheen which they still possess today, and which is indeed an extraordinary technical achievement.

Attempts were begun to reconstruct this technique: the few discoveries made are published, some at considerable length, in the voluminous literature on the subject. Theories that these murals were painted in fresco, secco, or wax processes were accepted and rejected

Fragment of a Pompeian wall painting

again. Ernst Berger, who first of all supported the wax painting hypothesis, eventually decided that the frescoes must have been painted in stucco lustro, and this is probably basically correct. There were then still two alternatives: either a coloured fresco plaster could have been smoothed very carefully and overpainted *a secco*, or the painting was smoothed when all the details—figures, flowers, etc.—had been painted on.

The most recent experiments seem to confirm that wax was not a necessary ingredient in the process at all, either for the actual painting or for intensifying the gloss of the surface afterwards.[11] In the author's attempt to reconstruct this technique the glossy surface was obtained in the following way. Both layers of plaster, the lower and the upper, consisted of similar proportions of lime and sand, the upper layer containing a little extra finer sand. To fix the plaster some brick-dust consisting of hydraulic materials, which effect a sintering process, was added. The uppermost layer of plaster consisted of marble-dust with a little sand. When this had been smoothed with a trowel a coat of stain was applied with a brush; this coat was overpainted with the ground colour and the actual paintings were then executed on this surface. The painting could then be ironed, either immediately or after a few hours' delay, depending on its moisture, and in this way it at once took on the characteristic gloss. The danger of the colours being torn off in the ironing was averted by mixing them with a little slightly alkaline soap, which made them more tractable.

Mural paintings executed in this way have such a hard, smooth and dense surface that not only does a minimum of dust settle on them, but they are more resistant to mechanical damage than any other surface produced by a brush technique. There is every reason to suppose that this technique was consciously developed with such considerations in mind.

The division of the wall surface into base, moulding, perpendicular bands, and columns was probably also a technical, as well as an artistic device. When it was a matter of painting *a fresco* and then ironing the painted surface almost immediately, it was much easier to work on small sections than on the whole wall surface at once. The secco overpainting should also be regarded in this light: it gave the desired opportunity to divide up the surface and consequently made the work much easier. The actual decoration was then painted in independently of the fresco ground. The style was here obviously influenced by the technique. On the other hand, the technique used for the decoration of these late Roman villas enabled the growth of a representative style in the best sense. The fresco painters of Pompeii succeeded in obtaining the effect of stucco lustro—successfully imitating the surface of precious materials—with very simple means and a cleverly constructed technique, and despite the considerable accomplishments of later times, we may still admire these works as a high point of technical achievement.

GROUND:	A variety of plaster grounds
MATERIALS:	Casein, distemper, or size colours
TOOLS:	Brushes

The term 'fresco' is often incorrectly applied to all mural painting, thereby stretching a term which originally meant only the process of painting on fresh unset plaster. But the so-called *secco* technique, or painting on dry plaster, has always existed side by side with fresco: the earliest works executed in secco were the murals of ancient Egypt.

Secco is in some ways easier to master than genuine fresco. The artist is neither limited to colours which resist the action of lime, nor is he tied to the 'day-piece'. The various methods of secco painting depend on whether size, casein, or distemper are used for the ground and vehicle: on these in turn depend the quality and intensity of the colours. Innumerable variations are possible according to the combination of ingredients: the grain of the ground, the nature of the vehicle (which can make the colours transparent or opaque), the colours themselves, all these combine to enhance or subdue each other's effect. As a result mural paintings executed in secco may look very different; the technique chosen must depend on the immediate purpose of the work to be carried out.

As secco painting derives its character largely from the grain of the plaster ground, it is important that this should be determined from the start in relation to the size of the wall and the character of the projected painting, for it is important that the wall structure and the painting should be in harmony. The wholeness of the wall must be preserved for both technical and artistic reasons and on this factor too the painting technique must depend. Two methods may be used. The colour can either be glazed on, or it can be used semi-opaque or as body colour, care being taken, however, not to disguise the grain of the plaster. If the artist wants the wall surface to be an active ingredient in the painting—to be a support in an outward and an inward sense—he will use colours such as casein tempera which can be glazed or used semi-translucently. In this method the plaster surface is not closed up; its texture is preserved and the faceted, exposed grains of sand themselves form the surface of the painting. The effect of the colours is enhanced by the strong reflective power of the calcareous crystals; the shimmering ground makes them insubstantial and very high in tone. The wall surface dominates and holds together both the painted and unpainted portions so that the composition can be very loosely conceived. The same wall, which reveals its character in the unpainted areas, seems to allow the forms to emerge from it in others, without disguising its structure. The combination of the wall's powerful 'personality' and the cool, high tones of the colours make secco an unsuitable technique for mural decoration which is to impart a warm atmosphere.

Hans-Jürgen Schlieker:
'Coal Forest', 1944. Secco
in casein paint, for the
most part scumbled

*Jörg Ratgeb:
Detail from the
wall paintings in
the cloisters of
Carmelite Monastery,
Frankfurt–am–Main.
1515–17. Secco*

Another, quite dissimilar branch of secco is practised with opaque distemper. In this technique it is not the grain of the plaster ground which constitutes the surface but a soft, matt, almost cloth-like layer of paint which completely conceals the texture of the wall. The colours are rich and deep. The influence of the naked plaster is eliminated in the finished work, so that the whole picture surface must be painted. Consequently the painting is isolated from the rest of the wall, assuming an independence which may entirely change the character of the room.

The appearance of the painting will depend on the choice of the plaster grain: the natural texture—a grained surface smoothed with a wood float—can either be left, or rubbed smooth, or roughened artificially by the admixture of coarse sawdust. A rough surface also demands a coarser painting method. This in turn leads to simpler forms and a larger scale, the painting appears softer and more substantial through the ground, and a certain feeling of space is created.

There is another secco technique which is particularly conducive to free, large-scale work; with this method distemper colours are glazed on to a smooth ground which has previously been soaped. The brush glides easily over the surface: there is no roughness to resist its progress. The brush strokes do not entirely disappear and delicate effects similar to watercolours can be obtained.

The different branches of secco have already been compared, in text and pictures, in a previous work.[12] Here we shall only illustrate an example of late Gothic secco, a detail from the decorations in the cloisters of the Carmelite Monastery in Frankfurt by Jörg Ratgeb, painted in fat casein tempera, and a modern work in casein paint mainly glazed but partly also opaque and semi-opaque. These two illustrations alone are enough to make it clear how much the variations in the technique influence colour, size, composition, scale, and warmth. The skilful artist will evaluate and make use of these variations as artistic elements.

FRESCO-SECCO (LIME PAINTING)

GROUND:	Polished lime-plaster
MATERIALS:	Lime-fast colours, prepared with lime-water and diluted with slaked lime
TOOLS:	Bristle brushes

The term 'fresco-secco' appears to be a contradiction and we must therefore begin by explaining what it means. Fresco is the technique of painting on fresh, moist plaster; fresco-secco means painting on plaster which has set. To ensure that the pigments will fuse as completely with the ground as they do in 'buon fresco', the surface is thoroughly soaked and washed down several times with slaked lime to which some fine river sand has been added. The paint must be applied while the slaked lime is in this viscous state. The execution should be free and 'dashing' and a good deal of skill is required not only in the handling of the paint but in making the best of a restricted palette and equally restricted range of expression. Fresco-secco is particularly suitable for light rooms and outside walls which are roofed in.

Giotto (1266–1337): 'St Francis giving his cloak to a pauper'. Assisi. Fresco-secco

The slaked lime has a strong power of reflection; the colours, already lightened considerably by the opaque lime, become even lighter when dry. White is the dominant colour in lime painting, but in contrast to the glazing technique the drawing and forms look flat, soft and cloth-like, and the colours are aptly described as 'milky'. This technique was especially popular in the Rococo period because, like pastel, which was then very much in favour, its tones are soft and delicate. In fact, the effect of a lime painting is best compared to pastel and the masters of both techniques—Watteau, Boucher, Fragonard, Tiepolo—resemble each other in their use of colour.[12]

The number of colours can be increased by adding casein to the lime; this also makes them more intense. If the amount of casein is still further increased, fresco-secco becomes lime-casein painting, i.e. secco proper.

Whether religious or secular, mural paintings tend to be used to represent serious subjects, and the painter usually aims, with justification, at a severe composition which will harmonize with the character of the wall. But there is nothing to prevent him from choosing a gay, light-hearted subject, or pretending that the wall is an opening into an imaginary room—in fact from letting loose his fantasy; in this way lime painting, once so frequently used, may still find a place in contemporary art and become the exception that proves the laws of mural painting.

GROUND:	Moist lime-plaster, in several layers
MATERIALS:	Lime-resistant colours prepared with slaked lime
TOOLS:	Hair and bristle brushes

Ingres wrote in his journal that 'The greatest masters always had a special predilection for fresco. Fresco painting gave them greater inspiration than any other technique.' Such praise has been constantly reiterated until the present day.[13]

Why this great weakness for fresco? What distinguishes fresco from other methods of painting? Firstly, there are the objective advantages of the technique. Fresco is very durable, and the colours are extraordinarily luminous, which makes them so suitable a medium for wall painting. Secondly, there is a subjective reason from the painter's point of view: fresco painting is a challenge to the artist; a 'thrilling tension persists as long as he paints'; he has a constant struggle with the wall, he must work quickly and accurately, he must be absolute master of the technique, and every brush stroke must be right the first time.

Despite the attractiveness of 'buon fresco' the modern artist prefers different methods, under certain circumstances, because real frescoes are easily damaged by the sulphurous fumes produced by modern industry. For instance the colours are sometimes bound with potassium silicate.

The technique which we now call 'true' fresco, that is, 'buon fresco', was first perfected in Italy in about 1300. It consists of painting with lime-resistant colours on damp lime-plaster, i.e. plaster which has not yet set. The plaster can only be painted on in this state, and consequently the painter divides his work into so-called 'day-pieces', each 'day-piece' being the area which he can finish in one day. When the plaster sets, the particles of colour crystallize into the wall and remain permanently fused with it. They cannot flake off as they can in secco; the fresco can only be damaged if the wall decays in some way, by efflorescence, for instance, or if the plaster flakes off. The plaster layers must therefore be very carefully built up. The fresco painter can only use colours which are not chemically affected by lime.

Although scholars are not agreed as to what extent they can be called fresco, variants of the true fresco technique and methods which are in effect early stages of it, already existed in ancient times.[14] For the purposes of this exposition, however, we shall restrict ourselves mainly to the typical 'buon fresco' used since the Italian Renaissance.

Since slaked lime is the only medium used, the particles of colour in a fresco are denser than in other techniques, are very luminous, and lighten when dry. The plaster constantly changes its nature during this process, consequently the intensity of the colours varies

Michelangelo
(1475–1564):
Head of Adam;
detail from the
Sistine ceiling.
Fresco

according to the moment when they are applied. These variations depend 'less on the differences between light and dark colours than on the changes in the crystalline structure of the plaster. They are the cause of the characteristic fresco surface. The correct utilization of the properties of fresh lime-plaster demands many years' experience.'[13]

Any experienced fresco painter will agree that new discoveries and surprises come to him with each painting he attempts. The rich and unique possibilities of fresco are exhausted only after a long acquaintance with this medium.

The luminosity of the colours is increased by their crystalline structure: light is reflected from the bottom of the crystals as well as from the surface. 'The light conjures forth a glimmer which can be augmented to delicate brilliance. This is one of the reasons why fresco has always been esteemed a noble technique, and why it is the best medium for decorating interior walls; walls painted in different manner may look sleepy and inert, but the fresco produces a constant play of light on the tonal values of the wall. The intensity of the colours though not quite so strong is similar to mosaic, another technique whose great impressiveness depends equally on light reflected from below the surface, i.e. from the bottom of the tesserae.'[13]

With experience the artist will learn that it is best to mix the colours with a little lime before use. Used in varying amounts, it helps to minimize the differences in intensity caused by the fact that some colours dry much darker than others. Colours mixed with a relatively watery lime have a greater power of reflection than drier ones, but the water must be added with care because plaster that is too dilute cracks when drying.

The chief consideration in all fresco painting is the setting time of the plaster. It means that the artist is obliged to paint one small section, or 'day-piece', at a time. He can only paint that part of the work which is freshly plastered, but he must complete this portion because in 'buon fresco' nothing can be added or altered after the plaster has set.[15] This time factor gives fresco painting an extraordinary vitality because it means that the brushwork must be quick, the forms monumental, and the range of colours limited.[16]

Since the fourteenth century, fresco painting has been simplified by the use of life-size cartoons which are traced on to or pressed into the wall. Even now cartoons are almost indispensable for large, carefully planned works. If no more than the essential forms are traced from the cartoon the artist still has the maximum amount of freedom and the composition will inevitably adapt itself to harmonize with the wall; the union of painting and wall is thus assured. An over-detailed, slavishly copied cartoon is obviously out of keeping with fresco painting, whose essence is in the artist's free and spontaneous approach to the fresh plaster.

Nevertheless, as early as the immediate post-Renaissance period the cartoons for frescoes tended to be worked out as carefully as easel paintings and were copied mechanically on to the wall. The technique became imitative, and the free, monumental fresco nothing more

Technical exercise in fresco, using motifs from a grave-chamber at Tarquinia

The six stages of fresco painting:

Above: 1. *The wall is thoroughly wetted*

2. *Left: Half the brickwork is coated with a thin layer of rough-cast*
   Centre: Layer of smooth-cast
   Right: Application of painting surface

3. *The cartoon is attached to the wall and the contours are pressed through on to the damp plaster*

Below: 4. *Painting on the fresh plaster*

5. *While the left section dries, lightening in tone in the process, the centre section is painted and the right section is plastered ready for painting*

6 *The cartoon for the next 'day-piece' is placed in position by means of a water-level and attached to the wall. The plasterer waits until the smooth-cast has been applied before he adds the final painting surface*

than a literal copy of the cartoon, and so merely a lifeless decoration. This explains Muche's passionate dislike of cartoons. He would like to return to the earlier method, in which the creative imagination and freshness of the artist—tempered by strict self-discipline—were saved for the execution of the fresco. This is the only way in which the tension character-istic of all good fresco painting can be preserved, because the artist is not merely copying his own cartoon; he must animate the wall by a constant creative struggle with the limita-tions it imposes on his work, a struggle which is renewed every day.

Since the fresco sets with the wall it is a part of the wall, not an 'addition'. If the technique itself demands breadth of treatment, how much more does the participation of the wall enhance the fresco's monumental character. Far from being hidden and 'silenced' by layers of paint, its living structure is an active and essential element in the appearance of the final work. The monumentality it gives to the fresco naturally influences the choice of subject-matter—so that a pastoral fresco with small details, for instance, would be an abuse of the technique. The most stupendous achievement in fresco painting is Michelangelo's ceiling in the Sistine Chapel, of which a small detail is reproduced here. The province of fresco is the serious, monumental work, in which everything is reduced to its essentials, and it remains unexcelled for this kind of painting.

GROUND:	Rough plaster undercoat. Thin plaster layers stained with lime-fast colours Fine-grain mortar surface, about 2 in. thick
TOOLS:	Nails, tacks, handles with watch-springs, etc.

Sgraffito is now used again quite frequently for the decoration of the exterior walls. The technique of sgraffito consists of scratching through a design on to a ground of variously coloured layers of plaster. In Germany its first ancestor of any artistic significance dates from the thirteenth century, but probably it was known much earlier as the simpler, incised plaster decoration of the peasants. In the Renaissance, sgraffito was rated very highly and competed with fresco; in fact, in northern Italy, Austria, and Bohemia whole façades were covered with sgraffito decorations, sometimes with copies after famous paintings. The technique was then neglected and revived only in the nineteenth century and more particularly in the twentieth. The word 'sgraffito' is derived from the Italian *sgraffiare*, which means 'to scratch'.

A rough plaster coat is first applied and covered with a layer of colour, which must be completely light-proof and impervious to the action of lime. This forms the ground. As soon as it has set, a coat of fine-grain mortar, about 2 in. thick, is applied to it and the drawing is then incised so that the coloured ground is exposed again. A great variety of tools is

Hans Prähofer: Façade of a house decorated in sgraffito, Munich, 1954

Helmut Lander: Exterior of a house in Darmstadt, 1953. Sgraffito with mosaic

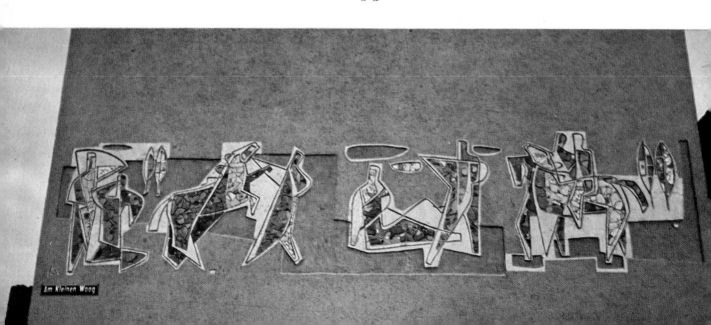

Am Kleinen Woog

used for this process. More difficult, and therefore less often used, is multi-coloured sgraffito; here there are several coloured layers, each different, and the surface is pierced to the depth of the colour required. The skilled artist should, if only for artistic reasons, be able to manage with only two colours. As in fresco, only as large an area as can be worked in a given period should be applied at one time, since clean and accurate results can only be obtained while the plaster is moist.

Sgraffito is very suitable for the decoration of exteriors, because the colours, being combined with the plaster, set with it, and are then completely resistant to the elements. Nevertheless the plaster, with the crust of sintered lime it develops, makes them somewhat pale.

The incising process used in sgraffito accounts for the fact that almost all earlier work in this technique is linear in character. Now a freer method is used and whole areas of colour can be laid bare. Naturalistic treatment is alien to sgraffito and should not be attempted; the strength of the technique lies in flat design.

Interesting experiments have been made recently by combining sgraffito with other 'flat' techniques such as fresco and mosaic. Our illustrations show a work in pure, multi-coloured sgraffito, a modern example of sgraffito combined with mosaic, and a combination of sgraffito and fresco.

Sgraffito
Intermediate Stage.
Smoothing the red
undercoat for the
second day's work

Technical exercise in sgraffito.
The ground is red and the
surface layer silver-grey.
The coats of arms
are added a fresco *while*
the plaster is still fresh.
The grey tone seen through
the windows is obtained by
scraping the surface lightly
with a scratching tool

BASE:	Vessels of raw earthenware dried to leather hardness
MATERIALS:	Clay slips of various consistencies: Ferrous clay slip for obtaining red and black. Non-ferrous clay slip for white. Ochre slip for violet
TOOLS:	Stylus made of hardwood for drawing in the design. Brushes

Vase paintings are the only surviving evidence of Greek painting, and until very recently the technique used by the Greeks remained a complete mystery. The two main styles of decoration, 'black-figure' and 'red-figure', were of course known: in black-figure the figures and ornaments are seen silhouetted against the clay-coloured ground, in red-figure, the background is covered with this rich black colour and the figures and ornaments reserved, except for the black lines in which the details were drawn in. There was also a smaller group, the so-called white-ground decoration. However, the exact technique which was used to produce these unusual paintings appeared to be inexplicable.

This problem began to be solved only a short time ago. We have based this account mainly on the arguments advanced by Friedrich Garscha.[17] 'For a long time,' Garscha says, 'German archaeologists have, for lack of a better word, used "varnish" to describe the shiny lacquer-like surface of Greek vases, although there was no doubt that the medium used in antiquity was not painter's varnish, which is oleous, and which, being an organic substance, fires out in the potter's kiln. Later the term "glaze" was adopted from Anglo-Saxon literature. But this is just as inaccurate, glazes being obtained by melting silicic acid—or compounds containing it—with fluxing agents at a temperature of less than 1000 degrees, so that they vitrify; under extreme heat a glaze reliquifies or at the very least becomes soft. The antique "varnish" however is fire-proof; it is also insoluble in water and unaffected by acids. Occasionally the word "engobe" is used, but this is misleading too because engobe is a coating of viscous clay which forms a matt and rather thick coating in the kiln. It is only very recently that the real technique has been rediscovered by physico-chemical analysis; it is in fact an accomplished form of slip painting, in which the differences in colour depend on differing thicknesses of slip and a single firing proceeding in several stages.'

The vases were therefore decorated with slip which, according to Schumann and Oberlies, was made by thinning down the natural clay with water and adding to it very small quantities of alkalis and decoctions of plant or animal substances. When this solution had matured the remainder could be poured off and used for painting the vases.

First of all the painter engraved the rough outlines of the decoration into the leather-hard vessel, using a wooden tool with a sharp point; the marks made by these instruments are still visible on all Greek vases. As, however, these incisions do not always coincide with the

Warriors in single combat. From an Attic eye kylix, c. 540–530 B.C. *Greek vase painting, black-figure*

finished drawing, it is surmised that the design was also drafted out in a more detailed preparatory drawing. Of such preparatory lines absolutely nothing remains; perhaps they were applied with a fatty solution which fired out in the kiln. After the application of the preliminary drawing, the whole vessel was covered with a layer of very thin slip which was quickly absorbed into the clay, and the decoration painted on top of this with a thicker slip. The thin slip underneath gave the vase a soft lustre.

The vase was then fired in the kiln. This firing was accomplished in three stages, which are distinguished by the amount of oxygen introduced into the kiln. During the first oxidizing stage both the thinly and thickly painted areas turned red, the latter becoming darker. In the next, the reducing stage, the amount of oxygen in the kiln was greatly reduced so that the thickly painted areas turned black and the thinly painted ones grey. In the third, re-oxidation stage, the grey areas turned red, but the black areas did not change colour.

The firing process was therefore apparently the same for both red-figure and black-figure painting. However, there was an essential difference in the method of decoration, i.e. the actual painting technique. Black-figure painting was particularly suitable for a flat, decorative effect. The black silhouettes are spread out on the surface; they are static; but it was impossible to achieve strong lively movement with this method. For this a more free linear treatment was required and in about 500 B.C. a new technique was invented through the apparently simple process of reversing the relationship of ground and painting material. So far the slip, which turned black in the firing, had been painted on the red ground; now the vessel was completely covered with the rich, lustrous black and the figures were reserved, so that they appeared red. With this method it became possible to draw in a

Boy with laurel wreath and crook, by Onesimos.
Attic drinking cup (kylix), c. 490 B.C.
Greek vase painting, red-figure

rich profusion of details on the reserved areas and so to satisfy the desire for a free representation of movement, particularly the movement of the human body. For the line is by nature dynamic and we experience its progress as an action in time—whilst a flat surface has a static and restful effect, a linear treatment is more suitable for depicting movement.

The contours in the finished drawing are raised and consequently are called 'relief-lines'. These relief-lines are about as high as they are wide and are clearly distinguishable from the flat lines with which the details inside the contours are drawn. They appear bolder and shinier in the deep, smooth black surface and their decorative value is greater than that of the flat lines drawn with a brush. They must have been drawn with a very regular instrument whose action was diametrically opposite to the free movement of the brush. Reichold described the relief-line as having a 'truly machine-like regularity'. Maybe the instrument was a single bristle fastened to a handle and dragged across the surface of the vase; in any case experiments tried with this kind of tool have yielded satisfactory results.

A comparison between black-figure and red-figure painting shows how much a new technique can do to bring to light new expressive possibilities. In the words of Ernst Pfuhl, 'The new technique gave birth to a new style.'

Red-figure remained until late antiquity a pure slip technique, but for black-figure, opaque colours were sometimes used. A third small group, mentioned above, was the white-ground ware, which also had coloured decoration, but the classical age preferred the harmony produced by the thin translucent clay-coloured slip and the deep lustrous black.

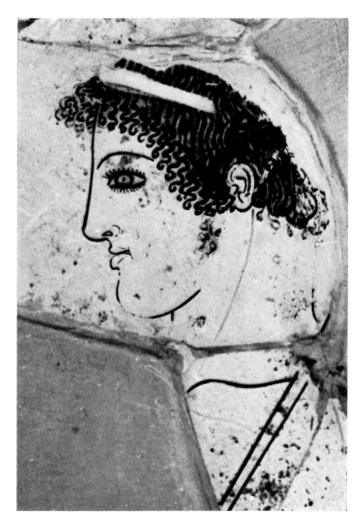

Head of Achilles, from an Attic dish, c. 470 B.C ; attributed to the Penthesilea or the Pistoxenos painter.
Greek vase painting; white ground

MAJOLICA (FAIENCE)

BASE: Biscuit-fired earthenware coated with tin glaze

MATERIALS: Coloured oxides

TOOLS: Brushes

All earthenware, with the exception of porcelain and stoneware, is porous when it has been fired in the kiln, and in order to make it watertight it is coated with slip or glaze and fired a second time. Glazes are compounds consisting of different minerals, chiefly metal oxides, and are divided into two main groups. The first group consists of lead glazes, which are transparent and mostly colourless, and so reveal the structure and colour of the clay underneath. Tin glazes, on the other hand, are opaque and completely cover the clay with a shiny white skin. Wares covered with this glaze are called 'majolica' (from the Italian) or 'faience'—the French name for the Italian town of Faenza, where the first Italian majolica was made. This technique may have been invented by the Babylonians; it was also practised by the Egyptians, the Assyrians and the Persians, and it was in fact never lost in the East. Majolica was first brought to Europe by the Arabs, who took it with them to southern Spain in the ninth century. From the fourteenth century onwards it was used in Italy, where it flourished during the Renaissance, and from there spread to Switzerland, Germany, France, Holland, England and Scandinavia.

64

'Albarello' (Italian
apothecary's jar).
Siena, eighteenth century.
Majolica

Although white tin glaze can be decorative by itself or tinted only with a little colour, it is at its best as a background for rich, bright colours. Painting on majolica proceeds in the following way: when the ware has been biscuit-fired and is quite cool, it is dipped into the liquid glaze. The biscuit, being porous, immediately absorbs the water in the glaze, so that the powdery white mixture adheres to its surface. The oxide colours are then painted on the glaze. Two kinds of colour may be used: either hard-fire colours, which are fired together with the glaze and include cobalt blue, manganese purple, manganese brown and black, green copper and yellow antimony, or muffle colours, which are fired on in a further baking and embrace a very wide range. The colours are mixed with water or oil before application and are therefore immediately absorbed by the dry glaze. Alterations are more or less impossible, so that the artist must have a very steady hand. Highlights and shading are put on at the end. During the firing the colours fuse with the glaze and form a glossy surface with bright shining colours. If desired, 'lustre' can be added later. This is a kind of paint in gold, silver, and copper shades which shimmer like mother-of-pearl; lustre was invented by the Persians, and is obtained by reducing evaporated metallic oxides or sulphides.

Majolica ware is sumptuous, vigorous, glossy and hard, and although it has neither the nobility nor the delicacy of porcelain, there is something healthy, solid and worldly about it. For this reason it was a favourite ware in the Renaissance for display purposes: the elegant dishes, plates, jugs and platters made in majolica were more for ostentation than use. This very fact must have influenced their decoration and landscapes rich in figures or architectural motifs taken from woodcuts or line-engravings were particularly popular. The most common subjects depicted were scenes from the Bible and ancient mythology, but purely ornamental designs were also used, especially grotesques filled with fantastic figures.

BASE:	Raw, biscuit-fired, or glazed body
MATERIALS:	Colours made from metals or metal oxides; coloured glazes
TOOLS:	Brushes

There is evidence that porcelain existed in China as early as the T'ang dynasty (618–906); in the fourteenth century it gained ascendancy over other kinds of ceramic ware. Chinese porcelain did not differ basically in its composition from European porcelain, which was invented much later: it was a compound of fusible white kaolin earth and fusible feldspar. However, Chinese porcelain was different in the respect that it could be fired at lower temperatures, and was therefore called soft-paste porcelain; besides, its glaze was more transparent than the European and was usually slightly tinted.

Chinese porcelain painting can be divided into three groups according to the state of the ware. The oldest process is 'underglaze' painting. In this the decoration is painted on to the raw clay which has been dried only in the open air (cf. European underglaze painting, where

Chinese brush-container. K'ang-hsi (1662–1722). Porcelain painted in overglaze technique

the decoration is applied to the biscuit-fired clay). Because unfired clay is not as porous as biscuit it does not absorb the colours as well; consequently it is possible to get clearer outlines by this method than by painting on biscuit. Only certain colours—cobalt blue and red copper, i.e. metal oxides—are suitable for underglaze decoration. This is because the porcelain is glaze-fired at temperatures which are so high that other colours would fire out. These metal oxides are therefore called hard-fire colours. The red colour is more difficult to apply than the blue, and wares decorated with it are rare, though in the Ming dynasty (1368–1644) we sometimes find both colours on the same piece. These underglaze colours are very durable because they are covered and completely protected by the glaze.

A far greater range of colours can be used in overglaze painting because the porcelain has already been glaze-fired, and they are exposed only to the relatively low temperature of a muffle-firing. The best colours for overglaze decoration are green, turquoise, yellow, and aubergine-coloured mineral oxides mixed with lead glass (so-called 'enamel' colours), and a 'dry' russet red and browny black, which do not contain flux. This technique has been in use since the fifteenth century and the overglaze colours were often combined with blue underglaze decoration. Sometimes gold was added too. As overglaze colours contain only a limited amount of pigment, they must be applied thickly for a strong effect, so that they stand out in a slight relief which can be detected by drawing a finger across the surface of the ware.

The third kind of decoration, in contrast to the other two, is applied to the unglazed but biscuit-fired ware. (Underglaze painting means painting on unfired, unglazed ware; overglaze is painting on the fired glaze.) This consists of painting variously coloured glazes on to the biscuit which is then fired at a medium temperature. The colours are separated from each other by narrow protruding ridges called 'cloisons', or by incisions. This is called 'three-coloured decoration', because three different colours are often used.

The technique called 'on-biscuit enamelling' is similar to three-coloured decoration. In this the colour is also applied directly to the unglazed biscuit, not, however, in the form of coloured glazes, which consist of feldspar with a large quantity of calcium, but with the enamel colours used in overglaze painting. This technique also requires only a fairly low firing temperature, but the colours are paler when fired than those obtained in three-coloured decoration, where coloured glazes are used.

The Chinese craftsmen obtained wonderful results with all these techniques as well as with others such as relief work and perforation; nevertheless, in later periods, their technical virtuosity tended to jeopardize the unity of the pieces.

The illustration shows a brush-container of the K'ang-hsi dynasty (1662–1722) decorated in overglaze technique with 'dry' and enamel colours; the decoration shows a number of 'precious' objects which are said to bring the Chinese luck.

BASE:	Biscuit-fired or glaze-fired porcelain body
MATERIALS:	Hard-fire or muffle colours
TOOLS:	Fine hair brushes

Almost as soon as porcelain was invented in Europe,[18] the first attempts were made at decoration. It is true that for a time they were limited to following Chinese models, but it was not long before the porcelain manufactories developed their own methods of treating colour and design, and the provenance of a piece can often be determined entirely by the manner in which it is decorated.

European porcelain is decorated in underglaze or on-glaze techniques like Chinese porcelain. In on-glaze decoration muffle colours are painted on to the raw glaze and fired on at a temperature of 800–900 degrees Centigrade, when they become permanently fused with the glaze. Being in slight relief on the surface of the glaze they are not as durable as underglaze decoration. The difference between Chinese and European underglaze is that while in China the colours were painted on the raw clay body, in Europe they are applied to the biscuit, which is then fired again in a glaze-firing. As biscuit is porous and more absorbent than the raw body these underglaze paintings never achieved the precision of the

Porcelain plate, Ansbach-Bruckberg, c. 1760. Hetjens Museum, Düsseldorf. European porcelain painting

Chinese ones. Even so, cobalt underglaze was very common in Europe and some beautiful pieces were produced with it; for instance, the Meissen 'onion-pattern', to mention only one.

The decoration is usually applied freehand after a pattern, with a fine brush or liner. Only purely ornamental designs are first sketched on to the body. In contrast to stencil-work, therefore, it retains all its freshness and spontaneity. The decorative element in porcelain painting has an appeal for many painters, and today even well-known artists execute freehand designs for porcelain factories.

SUPPORT:	Pieces of sheet glass stained with metal oxides and joined with leading
MATERIALS:	The same, support and material being one. Black solder for drawing in details
TOOLS:	Brushes for applying black solder

In stained glass the coloured glass pieces are support and material in one, and this distinguishes it from the techniques of mural painting. The picture is assembled from the pieces of glass, like a mosaic or a Pointillist painting. The character of the design depends on the colours and shapes of these pieces and on how they are arranged, while the graphic effect of the leading which holds them together, if vigorously composed, makes an important contribution to the expressiveness of the whole; the trellis-work of leading, black against the light, intensifies the colours by contrast. Figures and ornament are painted on with black solder in the simple lines of a monumental drawing. These drawings appear as dark as the leads and the two together constitute the skeleton of the window.

Stained-glass windows are known to have existed since the ninth century, although the early windows seem to have been decorated only with ornamental patterns. There is literary evidence for the existence of windows with figures in the tenth century. Since then the technique for the manufacture of stained glass has hardly changed except for a certain division of labour between designer and craftsman.

To begin with, melted glass is stained with metal oxides; it is then blown into cylinders and drawn out into sheets. Today any number of colours can be obtained, but the craftsman of Romanesque and Gothic times had to be content with blue, red, yellow, green and opaque white. Nevertheless the very powerful impression of these early windows depends to a large extent on being restricted to a few rich colours and enlivened by air bubbles, streaks and unmelted grains of sand.

The sheets of glass are now cut into the required shapes with the help of a cartoon the size of the projected window. Today this is usually done with stencils. The details, e.g. eyes, mouth, drapery are then painted on top of the glass with solder and fired on in a kiln. The pieces—which number anything up to 500 or more per square yard—are then attached to each other with leads, which are soldered with pure tin on the reverse side of the intersections. Finally the grooves of the leads are filled with viscous putty to strengthen the whole and prevent water from seeping in.

The unique quality of stained glass is due to the fact that the colours depend on diaphanous instead of reflected light, in contrast to other techniques of painting. The medium

'The prophet Jonas'.
Detail from a window
in the church of
St Dionysius,
Esslingen.
Gothic stained glass,
c. 1300

is hardly in evidence and the effect is one of a magical, coloured light. The effect which the ground or the materials have as physical substance is almost eliminated. It is the coloured light itself which we see, and in the last resort it is the colour alone, pure and liberated from all material bonds, which speaks to us with a magic power. No one who has visited the Sainte-Chapelle in Paris and stood surrounded by these glowing windows, can ever forget the wonderful, almost unbelievable impression of this flood of coloured light.

Elisabeth von Witzleben, one of the greatest authorities on medieval stained glass, wrote: 'This technique, practised exclusively in the West, was apparently invented by the Benedictine Order. Its spread is intimately connected with the spirit of Christianity, which opposes the worldly vision of antiquity with a vision of happiness in the life to come. Stained glass—magically lit up by the light of heaven—ideally expressed this longing for a supernatural life as no other art form could.' The art of stained glass therefore flourished in those countries—France, Germany and England—where the mystical longing typical of the Gothic period was expressed by the building of cathedrals. Originally the prerogative of the monasteries, it was later taken over by the laity and often used for secular themes. But although these late panels are of great technical interest, they circumvented the real purpose of stained glass and the attempt to use it in a naturalistic way was a failure.

The tradition of stained glass was only revived by the artists of the Expressionist movement, who consciously placed more value on spiritual content than on external appearances. Thorn Prikker and Georg Meistermann, a contemporary artist, should be mentioned as important modern practitioners in this medium.

Recently the Danish artist Palle Bruun has attracted some interest with a technique in which very thick pieces of glass are joined with reinforced concrete. The principle of this new method is that the thick glass enhances the effect of the coloured light; for although it is translucent, it is so thick that some of the light seems to lose itself in it and deepens the colour. Besides, the glass can be carved like stone, and the light playing on its surface is like the fire of a precious stone. This effect is apparently heightened more by reinforced concrete than by the usual leading.

Stained-glass window, by Georg Meistermann, 1955
Stages in the making of a stained-glass window
1. *Cutting out the coloured glass*

2. Drawing the contours on the glass

3. *Applying the wax contours*

4. Leading the glass

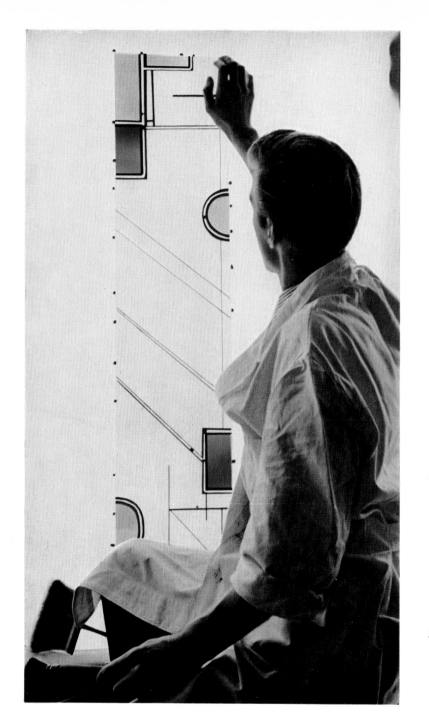

5. *Applying the patina*

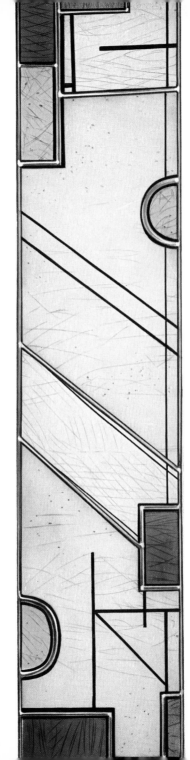

The completed window.
(The colour of the top left corner has been altered on completion)

SUPPORT:	Transparent sheet or bottle glass
MATERIALS:	Oil and watercolours
TOOLS:	Pen and brushes

Glass painting, now almost exclusively a peasant art, was already practised in antiquity, and there is literary evidence that it was also used in the Middle Ages. But it was not a common art form until the fifteenth and sixteenth centuries, when it spread from Italy to Germany, Switzerland, Spain, France and Holland; at this period it was practised in large workshops, which modelled themselves closely on trends in contemporary painting and often imitated in simplified form famous paintings of the great masters.

At the peak of its popularity, in the middle of the eighteenth century, this hitherto urban art form was transformed into the typical peasant craft as it is familiar to us today. The prototypes were abandoned, the workshops closed, and it was taken over by peasant families, who practised it in a kind of mass-production system. Glass painting was now chiefly used for the manufacture of holy pictures as mementoes of the miracle-working images in places of pilgrimage. Each of these thousands and thousands of glass tablets was a 'small, pious poem in colours, bearing the marked imprint of its creator'.

'The Flight into Egypt'.
Glass painting. Peasant art

Willi Dirx:
'The Son of the Magician'.
1953. Glass painting

Opaque and transparent oil- and watercolours were employed. The colours were seldom mixed, but juxtaposed in a glowing and sometimes dissonant profusion, and attractive effects were obtained by painting several colours one behind the other.

Unlike other techniques, the colours were applied in reverse order, that is, when the outline had been sketched on the details—for instance, the pupils of the eyes, eyebrows, decorations on garments, highlights and shadows—were applied first, the flat areas of colour and the background afterwards. Broadly speaking, the design had to be worked out in a flat pattern. A certain graphic effect might be obtained by incising the first layer of paint and filling in the incisions with other colours, a device particularly used in modern works.

The composition frequently consisted of no more than a few main figures with a little ornament; the remaining space was covered with mercury and the figures looked as if they were standing in or in front of a mirror. This 'mirror-painting', as it is called, was done entirely in transparent colours, carmine and green being the commonest. Sometimes the mercury—or metal foil, which was often used instead—covered the whole surface of the glass, the drawing was incised into it and the lines were filled in with black lacquer or soot; this was called a 'soot' picture. *Eglomisé* was a special kind of glass painting in which a black drawing had a layer of gold, bronze, or metal foil behind it.

Glass painting as a peasant art prospered for the last time in the middle of the nineteenth century, when it gave way to the advent of the cheap oleograph. Only the German Expressionists, stimulated by Franz Marc, revived it and even created some very fine works in it. Since then it has been occasionally used[19] but without widespread success. It may seem surprising that a technique which combines the qualities of unrivalled durability with extremely pure and glowing colours (absolutely protected by the glass from dust and dirt) should find so little appeal, but it must be remembered that they become as flat as the glass under which they are painted. They lose their identity as substantial matter, and only the pigment remains. The transformation of substance which is the mark of artistic creation and by means of which the artist elevates his material to a vehicle for intellectual and non-rational concepts—as for instance Rembrandt does with his mountains of impasto—finds no place, because the paint, being behind the glass, is compressed forward into an even layer. Modern artists, however, set great store by this physical quality of paint, and the lack of it in glass painting is not even compensated by the luminosity of stained glass, because glass paintings are quite opaque.

The glass lies on the paint like a coat of varnish; it is not as a material substance, smoothly applied to the glass, but as pure tone that it can have, if masterfully handled, that unique effect of shining out of the depth of the glass, and raise the painting to the status of a serious work of art.

Glass paintings have been called 'folk-songs in paint', and indeed there is something of the fairy-story about them, probably in part because of the way colours rest behind the glass, quite out of reach. The usual relationship between support and material is reversed; for the paint lies under and not on the support. If this element of unreality in the technique is allowed to influence the choice of subject too, as it does in the work of Ida Kerkovius and Lily Hildebrandt, then glass painting may be found even today to possess the means of conveying spiritual concepts. But a naturalistic glass painting leaves a slight feeling of uneasiness which is caused by the inward contradiction between content and technique.

SUPPORT: Small ivory tablet

MATERIALS: Watercolours

TOOLS: Marten or sable-hair brushes. Magnifying glass. Needle

The art of painting on ivory is restricted by nature to small-scale work. It flourished with miniature painting from the seventeenth until the beginning of the nineteenth century, the period in which the 'cult' of the individual created an enormous demand for portraits. Ivory provided an excellent ground for miniatures. Today this art is almost extinct.

A patron who chose a substance as costly as ivory for his portrait could hardly be blamed for not wishing it to be entirely hidden by the painting; besides, ivory has a fine surface by nature and a very attractive colour, which was also a very useful middle tone.

The materials used were light-fast watercolours. The paint was used sparingly in the flesh passages where the effect of the smooth veined ivory blended delicately with a mere breath of colour. Though the same materials are used as in watercolour, the technique for painting on ivory is quite different because of its small size. The colours must be applied in minute dashes and dots with the help of a magnifying glass; one tiny detail out of place—a dot in the corner of the eye or mouth, for instance—can spoil the whole picture. The brush

Portrait of a man, c. 1810. Miniature painted on ivory

is used fairly dry for this stippling technique. The free-flowing brush strokes of pure water-colour running one into the other are out of place, just as strong colour contrasts are to be avoided in order to prevent the picture from looking restless and bursting its frame.

The ivory is used mostly in thin tablets. When the surface has been carefully smoothed and cleaned the drawing is traced on, then washed off again, leaving only a suggestion of the lines to prevent them showing through the colours. The ivory is then covered with a solution of glycerine and gum arabic which makes the colours glossy and durable; in the flesh parts, where a gloss would have a disturbing effect, it is applied very thinly. The picture is now painted in the hatching and stippling manner already described, a method which can suggest modelling and subtle gradations of tone. The brush marks are not allowed to show in the finished work as independent elements as they do in a picture by, say, van Gogh. When the painting is finished it is very gently washed over so that the separate strokes are worked together and form a soft, velvety surface. If the colour has been put on too thickly in parts it can be lifted off again with a needle.

Sometimes luminous colours, vermilion, for instance, are painted on the reverse side. These shine through the ivory and other colours can be thinly glazed over them.

Broadly speaking, the technique of ivory painting is largely determined by the support; the ivory acts as a tone, it determines the size of the painting, it demands a quiet composition, muted colours and a painstaking precision in execution. Over and above all this, its physical beauty elevates the painting to the level of a precious *objet d'art*.

2

TECHNIQUES MAINLY

DEPENDENT ON

THE MATERIALS

GROUND:	Cement, mortar (matrix)
MATERIALS:	Tesserae of stone or glass

Mosaics made from inverted clay cones were known in ancient Babylon. In classical antiquity there were three kinds of mosaic. The kind known as 'opus sectile' consisted of relatively large plates of variously coloured stone which were cut in the shapes of the design; 'opus tesselatum' was made of small stone cubes, while 'opus vermiculatum', which is mosaic as we think of it today, was made up out of irregularly shaped pieces, long, square, lozenge-shaped, etc. This was a fairly simple form of decoration in the classical Greek period, whereas in Hellenistic times and under the Romans, veritable stone 'pictures' were executed in it.

Mosaic decoration was principally used for floors, but also for smaller wall decorations in the form of framed pictures strictly subordinated to an architectural framework. A decisive change was brought about in the fourth century by the early Christians, who decorated not only the vertical surfaces but the vaults, ceilings, and apses of their churches with mosaics. Mosaics covered the masonry like permanent precious hangings, completely disguising the structural framework of the building. 'The mosaics in the interior appear not to be let into the wall but to be radiated, as if from the house of God itself, and precipitated on to the walls, as insubstantial as a photograph projected on to a screen. Because the walls are entirely hidden and the bare structure may not show anywhere—in contrast with Roman mosaics which only partly covered the walls—the beholder has the sensation of being withdrawn into an insubstantial, purely spiritual world where gravity and solidity are unknown.'[20]

The mosaics of the early Christians were made of glass which is at once more colourful and lustrous than stone. Since imperial times glass had been increasingly used because it was easy to produce in a large variety of colours. The tesserae were cut off a slab of glass with a special hammer. In those days something like fifty colours could be made; modern methods can produce many times that number. Gold tesserae were made by laying a sheet of gold leaf on to plain glass and protecting it with another, thin layer of glass.

Now as then, the technique of mosaic consists of pressing the tesserae into a matrix of damp mortar, using a cartoon, the contours and the size and direction of the tesserae being arranged to emphasize the design and the action. This process is now considerably simplified because the mosaic can be assembled at leisure on the studio table. When it is finished, a sheet of stout paper is pasted over it, and it is cut into conveniently sized pieces which are pressed individually into the matrix. When the mortar is dry and the mosaic firmly in

Detail of a tiger hunt, Hadrian's villa, Rome, second century A.D.
Mosaic, 'opus vermiculatum'

position the paper is washed off and the seams are painted out. But although this technique enables the mosaic to be completed away from the site, it is a bad practice from the artistic point of view because the original spontaneous quality of the work inevitably suffers from such mechanization.

What are the particular expressive qualities of mosaic? To which style are the material and the technique especially suited and what, as a result, are the main tasks of the mosaic artist?

Mosaic is painting in stone, stone not only as pigment but as material substance as well. Each small tessera is bounded by sharp edges and its colour is unchangeable. Seen from the right distance the sum of the small patches of colour have the unity of a picture. Because of the nature of the material and technique the forms must be severe, reduced to strict essentials, and dominated by strong contours. This in itself means that naturalistic treatment is impossible. Moreover, since the tesserae do not lie on a uniformly flat plane they reflect the light in all different directions, so that the whole has a glittering surface with an air of unreality, like the sparkle of a precious stone. There is no soft graduation from one colour to another; it changes abruptly from stone to stone and from one tone to the next, underlining the mystery and unreality of mosaic.

This severity of form and the unreal quality of the light make mosaic quite unsuitable for naturalistic treatment, which abuses the technique because it ignores the interrelation of style and technique. Severe and almost imperishable, mosaic does not lend itself, as does the supple stroke of the brush, to depicting subjective or realistic forms. It is true that for a time the ancients attempted to copy very naturalistic paintings in mosaic, even going as far as to imitate the brush strokes; but this was essentially a misuse of a technique whose unique quality was strict stylization and a monumental rendering of form, and which demands and produces exalted, severe and ceremonious works.

Mosaics in this style are already to be found in antiquity, but it was the early Christians

'*Christ dividing the sheep from the goats.*' *S. Apollinare Nuovo, Ravenna. 6th century* A.D. *Mosaic in glass*

who discovered the other important attribute of mosaic, the power of the strange light effects to express the transcendent in visible form. To combine the visionary and the concrete was the task the artists of the early Christian churches set themselves, and mosaic provided them with a unique solution. At the beginning they adopted the antique tradition, but they soon abandoned the old illusionistic style for the strict hieratic formulae and symbols of a very concentrated form of vision. Their mosaics became a reflection of a heavenly transfiguration shining upon mankind from afar. The figures were represented in ceremonious, majestic frontality, strictly symmetrical and two-dimensional. The golden background, introduced in the sixth century, gave an added emphasis to the sensation of withdrawal from the worldly criteria of time and space. In order to visualize the impression these mosaics made we must remember that the early churches were only dimly lit by small windows. The only illumination was the light of the myriads of candles, which made them glow from the walls and even more from the vaults of choir and ceiling, like the heavenly Jerusalem, the city of gold, crystal, and precious stones. All the possibilities of the medium were explored and brought to bear in these early mosaics of the fourth to the sixth centuries —the most beautiful and most famous of them in Ravenna.

In the fourteenth century the art of mosaic was finally displaced by fresco painting. Its possibilities as an art form have been recently recalled and mosaic is now used to decorate public buildings of the more imposing kind. However, the modern mosaics no longer have

Exercise in mosaic, by the mural workshops of the Stuttgart Academy. Copying a stone mosaic. (Cf. prototype on left, a coloured photograph of the original in the Museo Nazionale, Naples.) The stones are cut and pasted on to paper. The boxes contain ready-cut stones. On the right are some 'day-pieces' which have already been provisionally laid

that evocative power possessed by their ancestors, possibly because of the differences in subject-matter, but also because very large works tend now to be made by mass production. Light is a vital factor in the modern interior—not candlelight, moreover, but cold neon or daylight which destroys that concentrated power which a mosaic emanates only when it commands a central position and light and space are subordinated to it. So it is only natural that close and severe settings are now to a certain extent abandoned. In place of the 'classical' mosaic we have the plaster mosaic and the tile mosaic. In the former, the design is set into the plaster—maybe on the exterior wall of a house—dispensing with background and border, but still a consistent composition in itself. A tile mosaic, on the other hand, is a loosely arranged design of variously sized pieces of glazed or unglazed tile let into the plaster wall. Gone is the closed mosaic field, and objective presentation and visionary quality have disappeared. They are replaced by a method of coloured articulation which can be both gay and stimulating.

Detail of illustration on p. 103. On the left, the coloured prototype; beside it, a mosaic hammer. Note that the duck in the foreground is in reverse, showing the underside of the tesserae, which will eventually be embedded in the plaster matrix

The completed mosaic attached to the wall, i.e. mounted in cement mortar; it consists of several parts fitted together

Professor Hans Kuhn: Ceramic decoration set in plaster. Studio of the Südwestfunk, Baden-Baden, 1953. Tile mosaic

SUPPORT: Soft, fine-grained paper

MATERIALS: Sticks of charcoal burnt from lime- or willow-wood

Charcoal is one of the very oldest materials to be used for drawing. There is literary evidence that it was employed even as far back as Greek times, and scribbles in charcoal have been found on the walls of houses in Pompeii. But for obvious reasons the earliest real charcoal drawings which are extant are of a much later date. For charcoal smudges very easily, and serviceable fixatives were not invented until about 1500; until then its usefulness was therefore limited to making temporary sketches for works in other media.

The best charcoal is burnt from willow- or lime-wood. Like chalk, either the side or the point can be drawn with, although a stick of charcoal cannot be made really sharp. Charcoal can be used as a linear medium or for shading flat areas; with both methods a powerful chiaroscuro can be achieved. On account of the structure of the material the clayey surface obtained by hatching with the broad side retains a certain linear quality.

In general character, charcoal drawing is related to chalk drawing, but although the 'grain' of a chalk drawing is almost always of an identical quality, that of a charcoal drawing depends very largely on the artist's touch. Although nearly all varieties of charcoal

Albrecht Dürer: portrait of the artist's mother.
1514. Charcoal drawing

produce a very black line if pressed hard, an effect of grey in a large range of tones is usually preferred, and all shades—from the very palest to the very darkest—are very easily obtained.

The artist can work as fast as he likes because he can make infinite corrections and alterations and his mistakes can be completely erased. As a result the technique has a certain looseness and grandeur, and is ideal for rough sketches; it has never been surpassed as a medium for compositional sketches and studies of details for pen drawings, panel paintings, and frescoes. However, as charcoal has to be fixed and detailed finish is hardly to be achieved with it, its usefulness is restricted chiefly to works of this kind. In spite of this fact, Dürer's magnificent charcoal portraits are the exception which prove that a truly great artist can cross the boundaries of his technique.

Ernst Barlach should be mentioned as a modern master in charcoal; his drawings, too, may be considered as independent statements, not merely studies.

Ernst Barlach: 'Despair'.
1922. Charcoal drawing

BLACK AND RED CHALK DRAWINGS

SUPPORT:	Paper, pasteboard, or linen
MATERIAL AND TOOL:	Black or red chalk

Chalk is found in nature as an earth of various colours, the varieties most used for the manufacture of crayons being black argillite and red chalk. Although this substance was already used in antiquity as a dyestuff, it was not commonly employed by artists until the fifteenth century, when it was popular mainly in Italy and Germany. Although chalk is soft and smudges like charcoal, it is not so sensitive and adheres better to the support. It is very suitable for chiaroscuro and for giving an illusion of form and was therefore a favourite medium with artists of the Renaissance, Baroque, and Rococo periods, who were sensitive to the plastic qualities of form. If black chalk is more vigorous, the red variety is softer, and perhaps for this reason it was preferred by that master of *sfumato*, Leonardo da Vinci. The two colours were often used in combination, the highlights being picked out in white.

The support may be white or tinted paper, pasteboard or linen. It must not be excessively smooth, else the colour will not adhere to it. A thin layer of starch paste sprinkled with finely powdered pumice-stone, when dry, makes a sufficiently good fixative. The point or

Hans von Marées: 'The Furies' (detail), 1886
Chalk drawing

the side of the chalk is drawn with, according to whether a linear or tonal effect is desired. An evenly tinted background can be enlivened with darker tones and highlights obtained either by drawing on or by removing the dark tone again in places. A drawing in several layers lasts better than a simple one, for the main problem in chalk drawing is the fixing, because chalk is almost totally lacking in any kind of binding medium and a fixative easily destroys its delicate pastel-like quality.

Both black and red chalk are better suited to 'painterly' work than to linear drawings; in other words, their particular expressive power is in a lively tonality expressed in broader areas of tone and enhanced by accentuated highlights, rather than in contours and lines. The undulations of tone obtainable in this way have a charm that tempts the artist over and over again into a sculptural treatment of form. This is borne out by the countless drawings of nudes which illustrate clearly how readily this medium responds to the artist's urge to describe form. It is the technique itself, melting and combining the individual small strokes into a delicate undulating surface, which stimulates the artist to bring out the plasticity and volume of form, and thus to use a naturalistic idiom; it was not therefore used primarily in the periods when art tended to be formal and stylized, but in those which responded to the magic of life through the medium of the living human form.

Michelangelo (1475–1564):
'Pietà'. The body of Christ is
supported by the Virgin.
Red chalk drawing

ORIENTAL INK PAINTINGS

SUPPORT: Silk or absorbent paper

MATERIALS: Ink wash

TOOLS: Brushes of wolf or goat hair, sometimes hare or badger hair

'It is difficult for Europeans,' says the Japanese art historian Kenji Moriya,[21] 'to appreciate fully the individuality of the brush line. Primitive painting invariably consists of contour drawing, and if a contour drawing is enriched with colour and shading it can give the flat surface an illusion of three dimensions, thus satisfying the artist's instinct for naturalistic representation; it is this which gives modern European art its realistic character. In the Far East, however, the contour line has developed its own independent existence and refinement and the illusion of form is suggested by accentuation and quick brushwork.

'From ancient times the principle underlying this brush-drawing technique has been called *Koppo*, which means "The formula determining the skeleton of things", because the artist must choose from the endless multitude of lines the one correct line which will suggest the skeleton. Superficial secondary forms can often enough be omitted. This is so to speak the linear interpretation of basic objective form, the individual creation of the artist; it can only be attained with the line of the brush.'

The great importance of the line in Oriental painting is due to the fact that in China wash and brush are primarily writing materials, and that in the Far East painting is a product of calligraphy and still connected with it, to an extent difficult for us to imagine. It does not therefore seem strange to the Chinese if Shih-Cheng, a painter of the Ming dynasty, says that a bamboo stem should be painted like the strokes of seal characters, a twig in the manner of cursive writing, leaves like ordinary writing, and the knots in bamboo like official script.[22] In the Far East calligraphy and objective representation are not opposites: both are read, and they are often combined in the same picture.

The shapes of objects are stereotyped symbols like the characters, and the artist must memorize them individually before he can combine them in a picture. These cyphers are not haphazard representations of the accidental, but the ultimate symbol, the last word: a tree is not a tree but the essence of a tree, a flower not a flower but the essence of flowering itself. They are not representations of particular objects: almost always they have some symbolic significance as well, which the spectator 'reads' as he looks at the picture. A rock, a flower, an animal is never just an object; every object points beyond itself to a domain of deeper meanings and associations. This alone would account for the exceptional spiritual quality of Chinese and Japanese painting. E. Grosse writes:[23] 'If you look at a number of brush drawings carefully you cannot fail to see that they are dominated to no small degree by the laws and ideals of calligraphy. To the painter as well as the scribe, the line is not only a means but an object in itself; it has, in fact, developed so far in this direction that its power to represent objectively has suffered as a result. The influence of calligraphy is equally apparent in the composition of the picture. The figures are mostly flat and are arranged not in space but on a two-dimensional plane, like characters in writing; plasticity is in fact avoided if possible so that the effectiveness of the line will not be lost. The connection between writing and ink painting is revealed at its most beautiful in the countless pictures which combine a drawing and a piece of writing, usually a poem, in one superb harmony.' Only in ink painting can this unique quality of the line be fully exploited: the undulations, the rich, live modulations of intensity, of direction and tone presuppose the Chinese brush technique. Even the more 'painterly' effects of some pictures, in which dots and flat areas of colour are placed side by side with lines, have been developed entirely out of ink painting.

The character of this technique is determined by the brush, the wash, and the support, whether paper or silk. The brushes used are mostly of wolf or goat hair, though badger or hare are also used occasionally. The Chinese brushes have a much longer head than European watercolour brushes, consequently they absorb more paint and the painting process is less often interrupted. They are made in a variety of widths and points. These brushes are held vertically above the paper and the wrist must not rest on the table. Chinese paper and silk are both very absorbent, so that a line once drawn cannot be altered or deleted. In addition there is a rule that no line may be drawn twice; the artist must therefore have a

118

Brush drawing on silk (detail). Japanese, c. 1700

very sure touch. As the paper is unsized it is very absorbent and an alum ground is used to prevent the colours from running. Silk is not quite as absorbent as paper, and has the advantage of giving the colours more brilliance. A certain depth may also be obtained by painting in the necessary parts on the reverse side of the silk, and this is probably the reason why silk was the more popular support. The silk was not always used in the same state; in some periods it was used coarse, in others fine, in some it was dyed, in others undyed. The colour of the wash varied in depth and brilliance, depending on the glue used for its manufacture.

Compared to black wash, colours (made from mineral and later plant dyes) were only of secondary importance, for 'the refined sensibility of the Oriental esteems black the most expressive colour. Black symbolizes the deep and hidden meaning of the universe: so the Chinese *hsuan* means "black" as well as "inexhaustibility of the essence of the world". The Chinese have developed such a high degree of sensitiveness to the possible uses of black that they can use black alone as five different colours. Obviously therefore no other monochrome can be substituted for it. Now there are also monochrome paintings in European art, for example grisailles and sepia drawings, but these are fundamentally different from Oriental ink paintings. The ink painting is made by shading with black wash; this of course is done with a brush; the ink and the handling of the brush are complementary elements in the perfection of the work, though the latter is the decisive element. The essence of Oriental painting consists, in fact, in breaking up the picture plane with lines.'[21]

THE EUROPEAN BRUSH AND WASH TECHNIQUE

SUPPORT:	Paper
MATERIALS:	Wash or sepia
TOOLS:	Watercolour brushes

In Europe the brush and wash technique dates essentially from the Baroque period. Its origin can be traced to the discovery of Far Eastern ink paintings, although it never gained the importance or esteem it enjoyed in China and Japan.

Painting in wash first became popular in the seventeenth century and its popularity was closely connected with the overriding artistic problem of the time, namely, a preoccupation with the nature of light, shadow, and reflected light. The contrasts and gentle gradations attainable with this technique met the need for a certain variety, though in the long run variety of tone alone did not satisfy the European craving for colour. In the Far East the esteem in which ink painting was held, was due on the contrary to the very fact that black and the gradations obtainable with black were considered the most noble colours. It is noteworthy that the Eastern technique was also different in that large areas were often left unpainted, so that the drawing itself had unusual gravity quite apart from creating an illusion of space. In Europe, on the other hand, the whole picture surface was covered with wash, leaving free only those parts where the paper was the highest tone in the picture.

Nicolas Poussin (1593–1665): Heroic landscape.
European brush drawing technique

The wash is applied with a brush, and in such a way that the light passages are represented by the light tones of the paper. Pen and brush are often used in combination, the
medium in this case being black wash, or, more frequently, sepia.

The brush and wash technique was revived at the beginning of this century at the time
of the Munich journal *Die Jugend*, and sometimes achieved a high degree of accomplishment
combined with a spraying technique.

WATERCOLOUR

SUPPORT: Colour-fast paper with slightly abrasive surface, or rice-paper

MATERIALS: Watercolours

TOOLS: Watercolour brushes of various sizes

Watercolours, i.e. colours which are soluble in water and bound with gum-arabic and gall, honey, candied sugar or similar substances, were known to the Egyptians in the second century A.D. We have the proof in their death-registers, which they illustrated with watercolours. Watercolour was often used for the illuminations in medieval manuscripts, and for colouring in woodcuts on the broadsheets of the fifteenth century. Dürer elevated watercolour painting to an independent art; and although other important contemporary masters made use of it, among them Bellini and the painters of the Danube school, their works have not the artistic significance of Dürer's. Although these appear so magnificent to us they found no true emulators in their day, and it took three hundred years before the technique was rediscovered, so to speak, by the English landscape painters, who adapted it to their own needs and painted great masterpieces in watercolour.

The technique appears to be simple, but in fact watercolour is a difficult medium because the colours are transparent and must be painted *al prima* without any kind of retouching.

William Turner: 'Venice after Sunset', c. 1839. Watercolour

Lyonel Feininger (1871–1956): 'Vision of a barque.' Watercolour

The paper has to be moistened and stretched before use, as otherwise it becomes wavy and the colour runs into the troughs. If it is used dry the ends of the brush strokes develop a hard edge, but on moist paper the colours are softly blended. Camel-hair brushes of several widths are employed; broad masses are laid on in a light colour and when they are nearly dry the darker details are painted into them with a pointed brush. Watercolour consists of painting dark into light and it is important to remember that the lightest tone in the painting is the colour of the paper. Once a colour has been laid on it can never be completely washed out and the highest tone is lost.

Watercolours look darker and stronger when wet; this is because mixed with water they reflect light, much like oil paint diluted with varnish. But when they dry, the light penetrates the translucent paint and is reflected off the white paper underneath; the colours must be exaggerated to a certain extent to allow for this process.

Watercolours have two specific properties which determine both the technique and the impression of the finished painting. The first is the speed with which the paint dries, which means that the watercolour artist must work fast and cannot permit himself finicky details. As it is almost impossible to make alterations, each part of the painting must be final with the first touch. The technique itself enforces breadth of treatment. The second important property of watercolour is its transparency, which makes the colours bright and glowing so that the light ground shining through contributes almost more to the character of the work than the painting procedure. Not only does the support affect the colours, but it is a colour itself, and, being white, is the highest tone in the picture. Watercolours appear to be entirely without physical substance, and their lack of volume excludes them from being used as a plastic element. They seem, on the contrary, to liberate concrete objects from physical existence; to convey an emotion of keen vigorous zest in watercolour is almost impossible. Transparency deprives the colours of the sensuous charm of pastels, although these lack weight and compactness too. The result is not, however, as one might suppose, an effect of aesthetic refinement or sublimation, although this might well have been the case with a medium so airy and luminous, but rather a spirituality of a more restrained kind, a cool, detached masculine spirituality such as we see in Dürer's water-colours, and, for example, in the work of the contemporary artist Xaver Fuhr.

The atmospheric quality possessed by watercolours makes them more suitable for rendering light, mist, and fog, than solid substance. They express concepts better than they represent material objects, to put it in a somewhat exaggerated form. William Turner's watercolour, 'Venice after Sunset', reproduced here, illustrates this power to depict light and atmospheric movement, as well as the 'sketchy' quality of watercolour—in the best sense of the word. Turner has completely sublimated the weight of the masonry and transformed it into a shimmer of light and water.

Watercolours mixed with white body colour are called 'gouaches'; these are opaque and yet possess the delicate quality of pastels. The term 'gouache' is often mistakenly used to describe modern tempera paintings on paper.

In conclusion it is worth mentioning some recent experiments with watercolour in mural painting. The first works of this kind were executed by Rudolf Steiner for the decorations in the cupolas of the first Goetheanum, at Dornach. So far this technique has only rarely been attempted. It requires a special ground which is very carefully laid on and overpainted with watercolours with a special medium which makes them soluble for only a short period.[24] When treated in this way they can be applied in several layers and produce an effect of great intensity and a translucency almost reminiscent of stained glass. Nevertheless, this should not be called watercolour, which stands exclusively for a pure *al prima* technique.

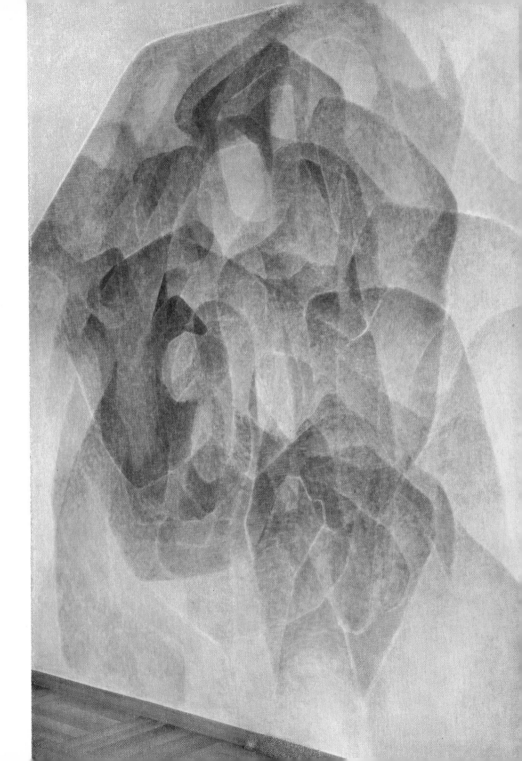

Felix Goll: Mural painting in watercolours; a new technique in which several layers are glazed one over the other. 1955

SUPPORT:	Paper, pasteboard, or specially prepared fabric
MATERIALS:	Pastels (artificial chalks made of ground white chalk and powder colour)

We know that pastels were already in use in the fifteenth and sixteenth centuries, when they served to colour portrait drawings sketched in with some firmer medium like silver-point or red chalk. We have examples of such works from the school of Leonardo da Vinci, while the portrait drawings of Hans Holbein the Younger are the masterpieces in this technique. Red chalk, which was used both by Leonardo and Holbein, is undoubtedly the forerunner of pastel, but pastel drawing only became an independent art in the eighteenth century, when it was also to reach its culminating point.

Pastel is the technique of drawing with a species of coloured chalks which can be used equally for graphic or 'painterly' effects. Since it is not possible to cover large areas with pastel the technique itself limits the size of the pastel drawing. The particles of colour lie very loosely on the paper and depend on surface reflection alone without the help of a transparent effect. If it were not for the fact that they must be fixed, pastels would be the ideal colouring medium because they are unadulterated by any form of binding vehicle.

Any form of fixative is bound to destroy the quality of pastels because it attaches them more firmly to the support, but though it will not crack or fade, an unfixed pastel drawing may disintegrate with the slightest touch or impact.

The great charm of pastel—and its technical advantage—is the ease with which the colours can be worked into each other: and by applying it in quick, short strokes the most soft, delicate, velvety tones and gradations can be achieved, this attractive effect being completed by superimposed highlights and accents. (Although working the colours together with the finger has the advantage of uniting them more firmly with the support, it is a practice which, for artistic reasons, should be used sparingly.) The colour effects may be varied almost *ad infinitum* by laying one colour lightly over another: whole rippling waves of colour and the most delicate coloured shadows may be obtained in this way, as well as subtleties of tone, especially in the flesh-tints, which are quite out of the range of other techniques. The strength of pastel is its ability to represent the power and intensity of light by means of the finest and minutest particles of different colours—not in contrasts of dark and light, or in whole areas of light tones contrasted with deep shadow. The cool and light tones are the most sympathetic; the technique seems bound to produce a light, graceful, almost playful treatment of the material. Stylization, dramatization, and grandeur are entirely alien to pastel, this is inevitable because what it aims at is, in a way, to disembody form and make it seem to float. The heavy compactness of plastic shapes is dissolved in a

Anton de Peters:
Portrait of a youth, c. 1750
Pastel

Adolf Hölzel (1853–1934): Composition. Pastel

delicate shimmering haze; only the magic of the surface is preserved, frail as a breath, a soft velvety bloom like a butterfly's wing.

A technique of this kind is by nature sympathetic to a refined phase of culture and so it is only logical that the finest masterpieces in pastel date from the Rococo period. It was an especially popular medium for portraiture, where these subtlest of gradations were in great demand. The art of pastel was introduced to Paris by Rosalba Carriera, the Venetian portraitist, where she was veritably overwhelmed with portrait commissions by the fashionable world. Her greatest successors were Latour and Anton Raphael Mengs. The end of Rococo also seemed to spell the end of this delicate technique, for it was pushed entirely into the background until Degas (and Menzel in Germany) gave it a new purpose in the second half of the nineteenth century. Degas's pastels exercised a strong influence on the French Impressionists; it is hardly surprising that artists whose main concern was the beauty of the outward 'impression' should have once more resorted to this technique.

SUPPORT:	Paper, canvas, primed wood panel, or plaster
MATERIALS:	Tempera colours bound with a variety of emulsions
TOOLS:	Brushes

The name 'tempera' is given to colours which are bound with an emulsion (a mixture of substances, some soluble and some insoluble in water) and stabilized with an emulsifying agent such as egg or casein glue.

Tempera is one of the most important media for both wall and panel painting, and it can be variously used for murals *a secco* or for portable panels, depending on the choice of emulsion. Ordinary egg tempera, very much diluted with water and glazed on a white ground, much resembles watercolour. If it is lightened with white, on the other hand, it yields a range of delicate, pastel-like colours similar to gouaches. If its oil content is increased the result is oil tempera. This is insoluble in water and must be diluted with turpentine, and when it dries the colours have a matt finish. A further step in this direction—the omission of the water and the emulsifying agent—resulted in the invention of oil painting.

Egg tempera makes an ideal priming for oil paintings if it is isolated by an intermediate coat of varnish. A mixed oil and tempera technique can be used to advantage: the oil determines the flatness of the background and details of form can be painted into the tacky oil paint in tempera. The effect of tempera colours varies according to whether or not the picture is varnished; many medieval works which the layman takes for oil paintings are in reality varnished tempera, for the varnish imparts a glossy surface and a certain amount of depth to the fundamentally matt colours.

Tempera is an old technique. It was used by the Egyptians and then by the Greeks and Romans. The Byzantine artists used it too, but they bound their colours with many different kinds of oil, some of which were non-drying, so that all Byzantine paintings have darkened and yellowed. Giotto, the great Italian painter of the early fourteenth century,[25] reformed the tempera technique in so far as he returned to lean emulsions which he applied to a white ground. He overpainted certain passages of his pictures in oils, especially drapery, from which developed the practice of painting in oil on a tempera ground. During the Renaissance and Baroque periods tempera gradually lost its importance because oil painting served the needs of the time better. The old recipes were brought out again in the nineteenth century and today the advantages of tempera as a medium are appreciated again:

Veronese School: `The Virgin in the rose garden', fifteenth century. Tempera

moreover, the development of new synthetic emulsions may open up a great future for this technique.

What, then, are the principal attributes of tempera? Firstly, the variety of painting methods which can be used, including application in layers, but not impasto; secondly, the matt limpidity of the colours, which give a picture in tempera a quality of solidity and dryness. Tempera may be handled with precision and it dries quickly. It offers the experienced artist many technical and artistic possibilities. Unvarnished tempera paintings on paper, framed and glazed, have to a great extent replaced watercolours, and tempera is the technique now most commonly used for rough colour sketches. It has still further advantages. It neither cracks nor yellows. Casein tempera can be painted on freshly plastered walls whose dampness would destroy oil paintings. Finally, if varnished, tempera can be overpainted with oils without trouble. But tempera must be used thinly or it tends to flake off.

'The tempera technique is characterized by precise brush strokes and must be practised

Ferdinand Lammeyer: 'Butterflies'. Tempera
First stage: The first layer of colour is painted opaquely on the primed support. Certain parts of the surface, which are to appear grey in the finished picture, are not painted. Contours, other lines cutting across the colours, and free graphic forms are incised into the wet paint

accordingly. Hence the use of hatching for the rendering of volume—as it was used by the old masters—is characteristic of tempera and also in keeping with the technique. Hans von Marées painted some of his works in tempera and varnished them afterwards, and he used the same hatching technique as the old masters.'[26] This typical, isolated brush stroke is clearly visible in early miniatures, which owe their vigorous, glowing, and untarnished colour to pure egg tempera. In fact this method of painting is essential with tempera, and overpainting must be done with great care, since the lower layers of paint remain effaceable.

Nowadays tempera is mainly resorted to, as Wehlte emphasizes, when the artist wants to paint with a limited range of colours, consciously avoiding a naturalistic effect. The astringent quality of the matt yet glowing colours makes them an ideal medium for this kind of work. Their opacity gives tempera paintings a certain static atmosphere, in contrast with watercolour, which imparts with such ease a quality of atmospheric movement.[27] The

Second stage: When the first layer of paint is dry, it is overpainted with a contrasting colour, in this case a dark one. This is then scraped down, so that what is not level with the first colour is removed again and the lower layer exposed. The remaining contrasting colour is sprayed on to enliven the surface. The incisions, now filled in, appear dark. If light contours are desired they can be engraved into the wet paint. The illustration shows the picture two-thirds completed. In the lower third the top layer of colour has not yet been removed

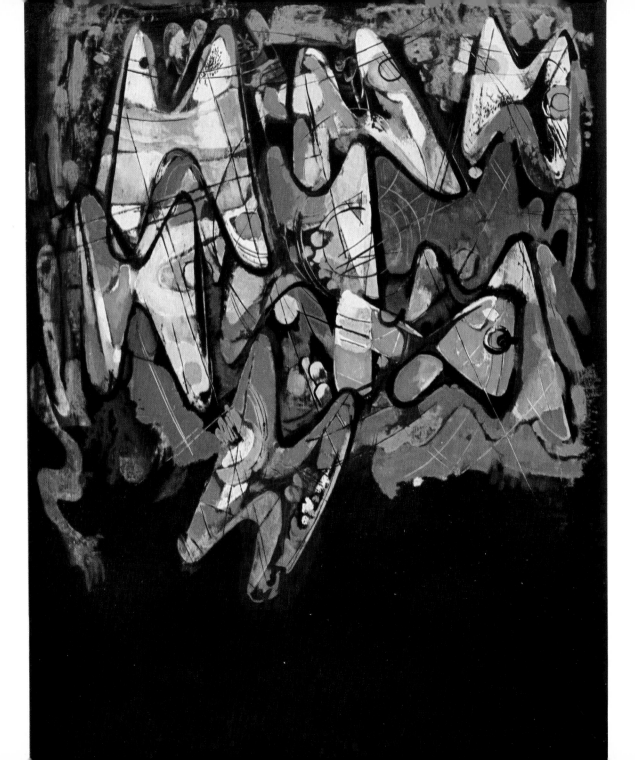

great precision which we admire also in the paintings of the old masters would not have been possible in oil paint; it could only be achieved with tempera.

Many types of murals in secco also make use of the tempera technique. The difficulties inherent in buon fresco led in about 1600 to an increased use of tempera, for tempera could be retouched and it offered a far larger colour range than fresco. It is also possible to detect where frescoes have been overpainted with tempera, for instance by the joins of the different sections of the painting.

Although tempera has so many advantages it is not an easy technique offering unlimited possibilities. Its chief drawback is that the colour values change with drying. If the picture is unvarnished the colours lighten, but if it is varnished the result is unpredictable. The general effect remains the same, yet, as Professor Lammeyer emphasizes so strongly, 'it is impossible to predict exactly what tempera colours will look like when varnished, even after years of experience'. 'Often a large number of failures must be overcome before the many advantages of tempera can be used successfully.'[28] That tempera is so popular with contemporary artists may be taken as proof of its attractiveness and its wealth of expression.

Third stage: The bottom part of the picture is exposed by scraping off the dark colour with a palette knife. The picture is now finished

This series of illustrations demonstrates the phases of a new technique in some respects comparable to sgraffito, in which very distinctly graphic elements can be combined in a predominantly painterly treatment

SUPPORT:	Originally: primed panels of wood; later: canvas. Also copper and pasteboard
MATERIALS:	Pigments bound with dry oils (linseed, poppy, or nut) and mostly thinned with vehicle ready for use
TOOLS:	Brushes

Both the Renaissance and Baroque conceptions of art demanded large easel paintings. The worldly outlook of these periods, in contrast with the Gothic spirit, gave rise to a method of painting in which the physical sensuous charm of the paint were fully exploited and which, moreover, enabled it to be applied quickly, a great advantage in a time when commissions were abundant. The fifteenth century marked the beginning of the predominance which oil painting has enjoyed without interruption until the present day. Broadly speaking, one may say that oil painting was a development from tempera, by way of the 'mixed technique' discussed in the chapter on tempera, which was used by the brothers van Eyck, by Dürer, Altdorfer, Grünewald, and other contemporary masters. The actual invention of oil painting is ascribed to the Venetians, in particular to Antonello da Messina.

Compared with tempera, a relatively intractable medium, oil paint introduced some important advantages and possibilities, both technical and artistic. It does not change tone

Peter Paul Rubens (1577–1640): 'Boy with a bird' (detail). Oil painting

Technical exercise in oil painting over tempera grisaille

1. *Tempera underpainting glazed over with warm-tinted tempera*
2. *This thinly glazed over and partly retouched with oil paint; highlights picked out in tempera*
3. *The finished oil painting. The different stages can be seen in the strips on the left*

Emil Nolde: 'Garden in flower'. 1907. Oil painting

in drying like tempera and watercolour; when dry the picture looks almost the same as when it is freshly painted. This enables the artist to see the final colour relationships of the picture while he is still working on it and so allows the painting to progress steadily. What is more, oil paint dries very slowly, so that the tones can be worked into each other without difficulty in very subtle transitions, and alterations can be made, if necessary. The opacity of the colours also makes alterations easy; one layer can be scumbled over another and some passages left completely uncovered. An oil painting can be painted either *al prima* or carefully built up in layers.

One of the most distinctive qualities of oil paint is its strong appeal to the senses, its brilliance and glowing lustre. Even the shadows need not be dull or matt: they can glow with a unique living colour of their own. One has only to think of Rembrandt: what an ideal medium is oil paint for his most subtle of chiaroscuro effects!

There is a great deal of truth in the claim that two qualities which oil colours first introduced into the technique of easel painting, namely, a quick sweeping method of application, and the possibility of making soft transitions in fluctuations of light and shade, contributed in great measure to the formation of the Baroque style.

The oil technique is unique in that it is possible to put thinly painted passages next to impasto. Impasto means colour used not only as pigment but for its three-dimensional quality as well. Painters such as Rembrandt, van Gogh, and Corinth quite consciously used real mountains of paint to achieve relief-like effects. The light passages in particular were accentuated by impasto overpainted with a highlight. A further advantage of oil paint is that it allows the artist to employ lively brushwork, which will make his individual 'hand-writing' easily recognizable.

It is incidentally almost impossible to speak of 'the oil technique'. Not only are there many methods of painting in oils, ranging from a very smooth application to daubing on the paint in a thick mass with finger or brush-handle, but a large variety of primings may be used as well. There is 'no technique with so many different sorts of priming. The variety chosen will depend on the painting method to be used; the purpose of a particular work will decide whether the ground is to be rough or smooth, absorbent or non-absorbent, and whether the canvas is to be fine or coarse. There are chalk primings, mixed chalk primings, mixed oil primings and white lead primings for canvas, and gesso primings for wooden panels.'[29] In oil painting the priming is especially important and has more influence on the appearance of the picture than in other techniques, where the nature of the priming used is comparatively unimportant.

The technique itself consequently influences the effect of an oil painting in several respects: in the glow and the lustre of the colours, the almost unlimited range of tones, the hardly perceptible gradations, the predominance of the colour, brilliant and 'painterly' in conception, and its value as a physical substance as opposed to line and form. Oil painting

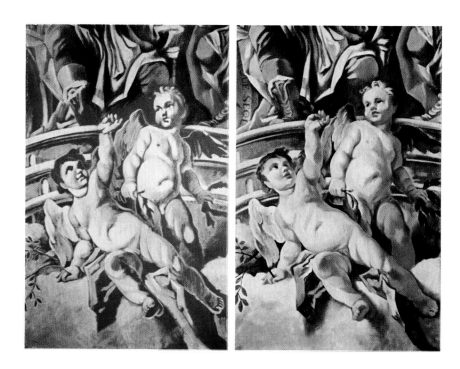

Reconstruction by Kurt Schmidt of a Baroque ceiling painting, Bremerhaven. 1955. Oil over tempera underpainting

Stage 1: Red bolus ground, with modelling in white tempera
Stage 2: The almost finished picture (detail)

The finished picture.
Oil on tempera

is a suitable technique for paintings of limited size, that is, for every sort of easel painting. In mural painting, on the other hand, the structure of the wall must predominate, and a naturalistic style is out of place. Oil paint is therefore quite unsuitable.

The beginner is tempted to take advantage of the opacity of oil paint and apply an infinite number of layers one on top of the other, instead of constructing his picture methodically, but a picture 'tormented' in this way will revenge itself by darkening. There are other dangers in oil painting: the colours may crack or yellow, and under certain circumstances they may even flake off. However, most of these dangers can be avoided if sufficient care is used; for instance, the colour should always be lean, i.e. with as little vehicle as possible.

SUPPORT:	Canvas
MATERIALS:	Oil colours
TOOLS:	Hair or bristle brushes

There is hardly another technique which has such a direct influence on the finished appearance of the picture as Pointillism or neo-Impressionism. This technique was practised at the turn of the century by a small group of artists led by Georges Seurat and Paul Signac.

The Pointillist method consists of using the colours of the spectrum unmixed, or at the most lightened with white. Black and all derivations of brown are excluded from the palette. Yellow, as the colour of light, is balanced by blue and violet, the supplementary dark colours. Colours darker than unbroken violet cannot be represented, but the artist does not wish to use them. All the intermediate colours and tones are achieved by placing small, mosaic-like dots of pure colour on the canvas, each divided from the others by a tiny interval of white ground. When seen from a distance, these dots or strokes of red, yellow, green, blue, and violet add up to a vibrant grey of medium tone; to make a light grey, the colours are mixed with white. If one colour is to predominate the grey is given a reddish, bluish, or greenish shimmer, according to the colour required. For good results the brushes

Paul Signac.
Boats in
Harbour'.
1893.
Pointillist
technique

Paul Signac:
'Boats in
Harbour'
(detail).
Pointillist
technique

must have a definite shape and should retain their size; each brush must be used only for one colour. The size of the brushes varies according to the size of the picture. This mosaic-like structure entirely excludes the personal 'handwriting' of the artist—a sacrifice which must have been hard for the successors of 'belle peinture'.

OIL PAINTING IN PEASANT ART

SUPPORT:	Wood
MATERIALS:	Oil colours
TOOLS:	Decorators' brushes, paint brushes of bristle and hair in various sizes

The oil medium is not only used for the fine arts in the narrower sense; it has also found great popularity in peasant art. The peasant craftsman is fond of bold effects, of pure opaque, unbroken reds, blues, yellows, greens, and white; he prefers oil paint because it is durable and washable and because it needs no complicated priming, protection or varnishing, and he uses it chiefly to decorate his furniture.

In the chest illustrated on p. 158, the decorated sections are represented as window openings. Simplicity of form and directness of colour are the guiding principles: hence a carnation is shown as a red circle with small white arc-shaped lines to indicate the petals, a tulip becomes an oval with yellow and red stripes and its leaf a serpentine line. Everything is painted directly on to the white ground in a bold, linear style: thick brushes are used to fill in areas of colour and finer ones to draw lines. The result is a gay, naïve, healthy piece of work, the oil paint providing an accommodating and simple medium.

Peasant chest from the Rhön mountains, c. 1780. Example of oil painting in peasant art

SUPPORT: Wood, stone or plaster

MATERIALS: Wax paints

TOOLS: Brushes and spatula (cauterium)

Encaustic, or painting with wax colours, was already practised by the ancient Egyptians, as we know from Egyptian paintings on stone dating from about 3000 B.C. It reached it speak in Greece during the classical period, and the names of the most famous Greek painters in encaustic, with Zeuxis and Apelles at their head, as well as descriptions of their master-pieces, have come down to us in literature. Unfortunately no specimens of their work have survived and the only remaining examples of encaustic are Egyptian mummy portraits of the Hellenistic period, which do not reach the perfection of the Greek works.

The formula for encaustic was lost in the Middle Ages. At the end of the nineteenth century an attempt was made to reconstruct it on literary evidence, mainly from a number of passages in Pliny. But the experts could not agree. Some insisted that the Greeks had applied the colours in a hot, liquid state, others that they were used in a cold paste and inusted afterwards. We may now assume that they were melted and applied with a brush, smoothed with a cauterium—a metal instrument resembling a spoon—and then inusted and blended into one another with a hot charcoal fire. The surface was then given an extra gloss by polishing it with a soft cloth.

Modern attempts to use encaustic have been much simplified by a scientific method which allows the paint to be liquefied and inusted electrically.

Encaustic has two outstanding properties, an unusual durability and the power to render natural appearances to an astonishing degree. Of the latter we have evidence in the famous story of the pigeons who pecked at Zeuxis's painting of a bunch of grapes, and we can still detect it in the Faiyum portraits. The explanation of this extraordinary quality is that the wax is almost totally transparent, so that the light penetrates it before being reflected back, instead of being thrown off its surface. This translucent quality makes the surface of the painting look like living skin, almost as if it were breathing. The mummy portraits of late antiquity still look fresher and more alive than any other works of art handed down to us through the centuries. Encaustic colours never yellow, darken or crack, and from a purely technical point of view the only thing which makes encaustic impracticable for modern use is the complicated method involved. Admittedly the efforts of the modern artist are not directed at producing deceptively real-looking pictures; hence his interest in encaustic is purely academic, without giving it a new impetus.

Encaustic more than any technique compels one to realize how much the artist's purpose and his technique influence and stimulate each other. On the one hand it allowed really

Mummy portrait:
second century A.D.
Encaustic

deceptive naturalism, on the other only those schools who wished to achieve such a degree of naturalism turned to encaustic, and only they were able to develop and exploit it to its utmost. Every age has its own artistic ideals. Apelles may have won a competition because he painted a horse which was so true to nature that a living horse neighed at his picture, but Franz Marc had a completely different end in mind when he painted his 'Tower of the Blue Horses', so that he had to use techniques which tended more to a spiritual emphasis. In the words of Professor Ferdinand Lammeyer: 'There is hardly any other kind of colour—excepting stained glass with its dense, almost remote radiance—which conveys so completely an impression of disembodiment. Wax colours used as a glaze are like a coloured mist: neither the paint nor the vehicle are in physical evidence. Used as impasto their purity and depth—in which the eye loses itself—can be compared only to the subdued lustre of semi-precious stones. "Der holde Schein"—outward beauty—is expressed by the word "colour" in the sense of a visible abstraction, without its concomitant of colour as substance, and quite untrammelled by the peculiarities which distinguish other techniques and influence—also from a technical standpoint—the artistic form of a picture.' Professor Lammeyer is right when he says that he perceives wax paint as pure tone, as opposed to physical substance, and accordingly to describe it as 'dematerialized'. It is curious that this 'dematerialized' medium should invariably have demanded a naturalistic conception of matter, and that it should not be used by schools of emphatically unrealistic tendencies. Perhaps every kind of artistic vision which seeks to embrace the beauty of outward appearance must lead to a new encounter with nature, a new 'realism'. Yet even realism does not imply copying nature but transforming and reforming it. The Egyptians wished to preserve the portraits of their dead for as long as possible for religious reasons, and employing Greek artists, they produced masterpieces in this durable and naturalistic technique which even today we cannot look at without admiration. But the ghostlike waxworks of bygone times, to take a negative example, are proof that this impression is not produced by the inanimate material alone, but that the material needs to be brought to life by the creative capacity of the artist. Though the wax images also give a deceptive illusion of nature they were only effigies, not works of art permeated, formed and animated by that transforming power of man as creator. This creative genius alone can elevate works in all techniques to a higher level, and bring about that metamorphosis which will turn them into true works of art.

BASE:	Wood, fabric, wicker-work, papier mâché, leather, metal, glass or porcelain
MATERIALS:	Lacquer, metal-dust, gold-leaf, mother-of-pearl, etc.
TOOLS:	Spatula, brushes

The first accurate information about Chinese lacquer-work supplied by excavations and literary sources dates from the fourth century B.C., although it is known that the art of lacquering existed in the second millennium B.C. Little has been preserved from this early period, but from the thirteenth century onwards we have many examples of what was by then a highly developed and very varied technique. The Japanese learnt the use of lacquer from the Chinese, but developed their own variants of the technique, and have great achievements to boast of from the Nara period onwards.[30]

Although lacquering, as an applied art, is all too readily dismissed as a craft, it is in fact a particularly good example of what is meant by a work of art being 'born of the technique', and also of the fact that technique itself is not something living, but that its expressive qualities lie dormant until they are liberated by the artist.

Far Eastern art can give us a particularly good insight into deeper perceptions of this kind, for the Eastern artist has a sensibility for his material which is the result of centuries of cultivation and which it is almost impossible for Europeans to achieve. To cultivate this

Kyōryū: 'Inro' (medicine jar),
end of eighteenth century.
Japanese lacquer-work in Togidashi
and Hiramakie techniques

extraordinary sensitivity requires not only natural talent and a careful training of sight and touch, but a particular mental approach. The Taoist conception of nature is that man should not master, force or dominate it, but follow and yield to it. This means for the artist, among other things, that he must feel himself into the nature of the material with which he is working, to liberate it and allow it to speak. Ernst Grosse[31] wrote: 'Through Taoism the artist of the Far East has been initiated into the secret of the relationship between man and

165

nature; he has been lent the magic power to give his material that rare life to which these decorative works owe their highly individual beauty.' The magic power to bring the material to life! Through this magic power the art of lacquering, which must have begun as no more than a method of protection, became in fact a fine art, even though technically it must be described as a decorative art.

The lacquer used in the Far East is not a synthetic product but is obtained from a special tree, the *Rhus vernicifera*. It can be dyed in various colours; it dries in damp air and is unusually resistant. The lacquer is applied to the support in many layers, each very thin, and each layer must be dry before the next is superposed. The ground must be very carefully applied: in really good Chinese or Japanese lacquer-work the ground alone takes anything up to thirty processes. This procedure can be summarized as follows: first the processing of the wood base,[22] then the covering of the base with linen, and finally the application, drying, and polishing of the lower and middle layers of lacquer. Almost all lacquering techniques are built up on this foundation.

We can do no more than select a few of the most important techniques used for decorating lacquer-ware. It should be noted that in Japan, contrary to the Chinese custom, lacquer is very seldom used as a binding medium for the colours or gold-dust. Nearly all Japanese lacquer-work is executed in the *makie* technique, which means, translated literally, 'scattered picture'. The gold-dust or coloured lacquer powder is sprinkled into the damp lacquer drawing, which differs according to size and density. A painted lacquer picture, executed in a technique analogous to oil painting, with lacquer as the medium, is called *Urushi-e*.

There are a large number of techniques; they are distinguished by the substance sprinkled or laid into the lacquer, whether it be fine powder, gold-dust, gold inlays of various sizes—and the further treatment, consisting either of coating with clear varnish, polishing, coating again, etc. *Nashiji*, *Ikakeji*, *Kinji*, and *Shibuichi-ji* are the names of various grounds used (coarse or fine, smooth and lustrous gold ground, and a silver-grey ground respectively); *Togidashi*, *Hiramakie*, and *Takamakie* are techniques for the actual decoration (a kind of highly polished lacquer and a flat or modelled 'scattered picture'). The effect of the lacquer is enriched and accentuated with mother-of-pearl, coral, lead, and other inlays. Another technique consists of incising the lacquer ground and rubbing gold into the lines; this is the so-called *Chinkinbori* technique. The areas enclosed by the lines are sometimes filled in with colour.

The Coromandel technique is a combination of relief-work and painting. The wood base is coated with a layer of chalk or clay and covered with black lacquer. When this is completely dry the picture is cut out of the lacquer in intaglio in much the same way as a woodcut, so that the chalk is exposed. These exposed areas are then painted in with strong watercolours. The contours and other lines remain as raised cloisons. The particular charm

167

*Screen, Chinese,
beginning of the eighteenth
century. Coromandel*

Lacquered chest (detail), Japanese. c. 1700. Coloured lacquer on black lacquer ground

of Coromandel work lies in the combination of the intense, glowing colours and the dark lustre of the lacquer.

Whatever technique is used, the lacquer itself forms a highly decorative element. It is like a polished skin, partly translucent and partly opaque, and it enhances the effectiveness of the piece and gives it an air of costliness. Lacquer is particularly effective on slightly curved surfaces; in fact it actually needs a curved surface, because only then can the light play round its reflecting shape. Even the modern lacquer painter prefers a curved surface in order to bring out all the qualities of the material, and it is presumably not pure coincidence that box lids and fronts of drawers were curved in the Far East, when they might just as well have been flat; the forms were simply developed out of the lacquer technique.

It is essential that the lacquered decoration should be in keeping with the shape of the base; a simple rectangular box needs in fact quite a different kind of decoration from, say, a round dish with a curved rim. The decorativeness of the lacquer, its subordination to, and accentuation of, the shape of the base are best brought out by objects of this kind.

On some objects the decoration, which should be subordinate, was overdone at the expense of the shape. The technique was, in fact, overstretched and ignored the fact that, like every other painting technique, the best results were obtained only within certain limits. These pieces emphasize the importance of the fact that the artist must understand not only the expressive possibilities but the limitations of his technique as well.

PAINTING WITH COLOURS DISPERSED
IN SYNTHETIC RESIN

SUPPORT: Plaster, wood, fabric, metal

MATERIALS: Synthetic resin with pigments

TOOLS: Hair and bristle brushes, spatula, palette knife

Besides the 'historical' painting methods discussed so far, there is a new technique which has become increasingly important in recent years. This is the use of synthetic resin as a binding medium for colours, particularly in the form of a thick impasto. The surface of a painting can be given much more richness with this material than painting in impasto with oil colours. The synthetic resin can be mixed with any colour and it can be painted in layers or overpainted with pigments containing other media, for instance, nitro-enamels.

This resin will adhere to any support and has very good covering and filling capacity, so that it makes an excellent painting ground. It may be smoothed with a spatula, polished down, or given any degree of roughness. It can be cut and incised and its absorbency can be varied as required. Any of the usual techniques can be used to paint on a synthetic resin ground, including watercolour, tempera, oil painting, casein painting, pastel, etc.

But the full scope of this material is revealed only when it serves as the painting material itself, not merely as the ground. (It can, incidentally, be tinted in all shades of colour, but not with all kinds of pigment.) It has many possibilities as a 'plastic' painting material: apart from the usual impasto brush strokes the layers of colour can be applied in a relief-like manner, or applied in several differently coloured layers, and ground down, or cut in a similar way to a wood- or lino-cut, and given an almost graphic effect. Something resembling a sgraffito effect can also be obtained by applying alternating layers of colour and wax and incising the surface to the wanted depth and colour. The top layers can then be simply lifted off as required. The resin can also be worked in thick pieces as a kind of mosaic; multi-coloured decorations painted on sheets of resin can be finished in the studio like a mosaic and simply mounted into the wall.

The possibilities of this versatile material—which can be used simply as pigment as well as for a modelled surface—have by no means been exhausted. So far it has been used rather for its decorative than its strictly artistic potentialities and the attempts made so far tend to be rather experimental, but it is quite possible that once the experimental stage has been overcome, synthetic resin will be used for producing serious works of art

Willi Kannenberg: 'Plant metamorphosis', 1955.
Painting with intaglio and relief, in synthetic resin

Sheet of studies in synthetic resin
First state: Multi-coloured painting in thick impasto; the surface is rubbed down while wet until it is smooth
(Note two sheets of abrasive paper in foreground)

Second state: In the areas which have previously been rubbed with wax the thick covering of plastic film can be removed again by cutting the contours with a sharp knife

Third state: The pieces which have been lifted off are cut up into smaller shapes and painted, partly in impasto, and stuck on to the surface with paste

Willi Kannenberg: Sheet of studies in synthetic resin
*Final state: The plant form on the left is painted in impasto with a palette knife, the one on the right is painted thinly
on to the wet under paint with plastic paint containing sand. The three panels at the top are sunk into the surface; those
below are mounted on it*

3 | *TECHNIQUES MAINLY*

DEPENDENT ON

THE TOOLS

PAINTING ON BARK-CLOTH

SUPPORT:	Bast fibres
MATERIALS:	Colours obtained from plants (red, yellow, brown, black); occasionally, earth colours
TOOLS:	Wooden liners, often serrated; dies, stamps, brushes made from bunches of grass roots

Painting on bark-cloth, or *tapa*-work, is a technique used in the islands of the Pacific Ocean, the most beautiful examples being found in Hawaii, Tahiti, Samoa, and the Fiji Islands. Bark-cloth has now been largely replaced by imported textiles, particularly calico, and in some places it is already a lost art.

Bark-cloth is used for garments, blankets, and bed covers, as well as for coating dancing masks and similar objects. It is neither a fabric nor wicker-work; it consists of the inner bark fibres of certain trees, for instance, the paper mulberry, fig, Pipturus, etc., which are soaked, laid on top of each other in uniform thicknesses and beaten with wooden clubs. Through beating and the action of a sticky juice in the fibres, they become matted and form bark-cloth. The thickness of the stuff can be varied by the preliminary treatment, and may range from the consistency of fine lawn to a coarse, tough and almost leather-like cloth. Already in the course of preparation the bark-cloth assumes the texture of cloth, the last beating being performed with a rectangular mallet of very hard wood with an artfully scored design on its surface. The 'water-mark' which the mallet leaves on the cloth serves as an insignia of family and property. The cloth is laid on beating boards with delicate linear designs incised into them, and as it is turned and shifted during the beating it takes on an almost crêpe-like appearance. A corded texture can be obtained by rolling the damp material with rippled hand-rollers.

The natural colour of bark-cloth is light straw, becoming absolutely white when bleached. But this light colour is not always suitable and, moreover, the islanders are fond of gay colour and pattern, so the bark-cloth is dyed and decorated. If it is to be uniformly dyed it is dipped in a coloured broth between beatings, dried, rinsed in brine to fix the colours, and beaten again. After the final drying more painted decoration is often added. The making of *tapas* used to be the work of the women and, although they only had few colours and very primitive instruments at their disposal, the designs are rich and varied and no two *tapas* are alike. Only at first sight do the designs appear to be purely geometric: as their names show, they are actually highly simplified pictorial symbols derived from the land and sea creatures, and the plants familiar to the islanders, and which include flying foxes, centipedes, triangular sharks' teeth, and so forth.

The instruments most commonly used are wooden liners, often with several fork-like serrations so that several parallel lines can be drawn at once. Stamps and dies are also used,

tail of Samoan
a' Painting
bark-cloth

the design being rubbed through the cloth; sometimes it is painted freehand with a finger, with small sticks or with brushes of various sizes. The range of colours is limited; most common are russet red, yellow, brown-black, and the natural colour of the cloth. Blue and green, which fade quickly, are used more rarely.

The technique of *tapa*-work has developed out of the tools. There are constant repetitions and new combinations of fixed motifs, but thanks to the inventiveness of the South Sea Islanders the designs have not become stereotyped. The texturing of the material also contributed to the final effect.

SUPPORT:	Paper grounded with bone-dust, and tinted
TOOL AND MATERIAL:	Silverpoint

Silverpoint was already known to the Romans as other metal points were, and probably used for writing on parchment which was polished with pumice-stone. The earliest mention of silverpoint as a drawing medium is in about 1400 in Italy, and some very beautiful silverpoint drawings from the fifteenth and sixteenth centuries are still extant.

Silverpoint was preferred because it was cheaper than gold and because it produced a fine, clear line. The point—mounted on a metal stylus—is remarkably fine and wears relatively little with use. The colour content of silverpoint is not very high and the line has a silver-grey tone, which soon becomes brown through oxidation. Dark lines can only be obtained by working over the same place several times, and flat areas of shade by close parallel or cross-hatching. The silverpoint line is indelible, so that corrections are impossible, and its handling therefore requires great skill.

Like all metal points except soft lead, silverpoint leaves no mark on ordinary paper, and in order to force it to deposit the silver the paper must have an abrasive ground; bone-dust mixed with size-water and applied in the form of a thin liquid is mostly used for this purpose. Cennini has left detailed recipes for the grounding of paper. The practice of tinting the ground in order to achieve more plasticity by heightening the drawing with white began quite early. The northern countries preferred an off-white tone for this purpose, while the Italians used first a delicate green and later also red, grey, and blue grounds. On the other hand, Dürer also drew on coloured grounds and Raphael on a white ground. When a coloured ground was used, the light passages were often heightened with white body colour in order to accentuate the contrasts between light and shade.

Dürer was one of the great German masters of silverpoint. He was not the son of a goldsmith in vain; the love of finely drawn lines and careful detail—combined in him with grandeur of conception—was inborn, and for this reason he had a predilection for silverpoint. His self-portrait at the age of thirteen, the earliest drawing by him we know, and a drawing of an angel playing the lute of which a detail is reproduced here, are both in silverpoint, the latter on grey paper. Dürer began by making a rough outline drawing; but he did not then follow it precisely and it is still visible, since he did not entirely succeed in deleting it. The broad and close hatching which he used according to the tone required is also clearly visible. Not content with the limited range of contrast he could obtain in this way, Dürer heightened his drawing with white, which he applied with small brush strokes to resemble drawing. This reproduction tells us several things about silverpoint: first of all,

Albrecht Dürer:
'Angel playing the lute' (detail). 1491.
Silverpoint drawing.
Berlin, Kupferstichkabinett

that it is a delicate, clear, precise medium. Its element is the isolated line, whose range of expression is in direct contrast to chalk and charcoal, which is soft and easily smudged and is the most 'painterly' drawing medium, and more suitable for articulating planes, i.e. for laying down tones. The silverpoint makes for a painstaking exactness, a kind of chasing technique; it has the small-scale precision of the old masters, as opposed to the broadness and freedom of a sketch. A silverpoint drawing is built up from innumerable individual lines, each of equal value, which do not permit spontaneity or strong emotion. It possesses a delicate and cool detachment, something of the frailty and preciousness of filigree.

SUPPORT:	Paper
TOOLS:	Lead pencils, ranging from hard to soft

Pencil drawing as we know it only dates from the end of the eighteenth century, when the Frenchman Conté in 1790 invented the process of manufacturing pencils of various degrees of hardness from viscous graphite mixed with clay. The words 'lead pencil' are therefore deceptive (since all modern pencils are made from graphite) and originate in the time when real lead was used, partly combined with other metals like tin or bismuth.

Cennini[33] describes a pencil which consists of two parts of lead and one part of tin and which gave a smooth, regular line of not very great strength. Lead pencils were treasured in the fifteenth and sixteenth centuries for making preliminary drawings for pen, brush, and black and red chalk, for which purpose they were very suitable, since the lead left only a faint mark on unprimed paper. Silverpoint, on the other hand, could only be used on a grounded paper. Pencil drawings as independent works hardly existed at this time.

The vigorous Baroque style had no use for the lead stylus except for making preparatory sketches. For this purpose lead was replaced in about 1600 by the graphite pencil, the forerunner of the modern pencil.[34] When exactly the graphite pencil was invented, or whether it originated in England, Belgium, or Spain is not certain. There is no mention of it until the second half of the sixteenth century, when it is described as a new writing instrument. It seems to have passed from a writing to a sketching instrument within a few decades, for in 1599 we find it praised as a medium for sketches for pen and ink drawings. The early graphite pencils were soft and smudgy and not very suitable for finished work.

The hardest variety of modern pencil makes a line not very different from the silverpoint, the softest not unlike that of black chalk. The softer the graphite, i.e. the less clay it contains, the more colour it deposits on the paper and the more easily it smudges; and the lines made by a soft pencil can be combined to form flat tones. The point of the pencil can either be sharpened or left blunt. A hard pencil is used for a draughtsmanlike technique, a soft one for a more 'painterly' effect; and the quality of the paper, smooth, rough or grained, also makes a considerable contribution to the final result. The pencil can be used for a large variety of work—from rough sketches to accurate finished drawings, for pure line drawings and chiaroscuro. The technique itself is therefore not responsible for any particular style. The pencil line is generally comparatively thin and grey rather than black, and both the colour and line are responsible for a certain element of reticence. This can result in a delicate, intimate effect as we see in the drawing by Chodowiecki, reproduced here, or in the work of the modern artist Georg Muche. It is also very suitable for a cool, detached style, as we see in the many pencil drawings of the 'classical' period. Rich effects and sharp contrasts, on the other hand, are beyond the scope of the pencil.

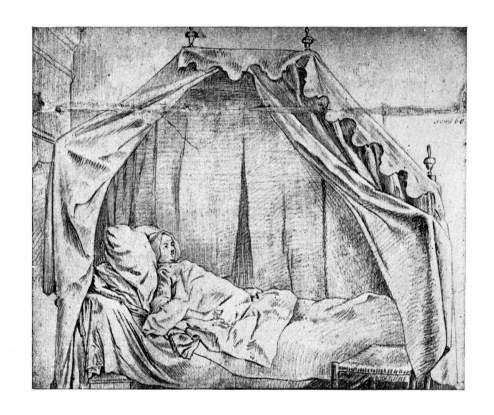

Daniel Chodowiecki (1726–1801): 'Woman resting'. Pencil drawing. Berlin, Kupferstichkabinett

SUPPORT:	Strong, absorbent paper with smooth surface
MATERIALS:	Ink or wash or sepia (the last only since the eighteenth century)
TOOL:	Quill, reed, or steel pen

Pens have been used as writing instruments since ancient times, and pen drawings, often coloured, have existed for a very long time as accompaniments to written or printed texts. But in the form of independent graphic works they only date from the beginning of the Middle Ages; the Utrecht Psalter of the ninth century is an early example.

For these early pen drawings the kind of pen most frequently used was the quill, which is cut from the pinion feathers of birds. The reed pen, though older than the quill, did not become common until artists like Rembrandt used it in the seventeenth century. The steel pen was invented in the nineteenth century and has been the most usual kind until the present day. The choice of pen depends on the type of drawing to be made and on the artist's temperament. A steel pen can be absolutely controlled and is infallibly accurate. It draws a sober, factual line which conveys no more and no less than what the artist wishes to express. On the other hand the quill or the reed produces certain accidental qualities which cannot be anticipated, but, if taken advantage of, can impart a certain uniqueness to the drawing. This is quite apart from the great variety obtainable by using nibs of different sizes, which may produce anything from extremely fine, spidery traces to broad, full

Rembrandt (1606–69): 'Woman in an armchair, reading'. Pen drawing

strokes. One is almost tempted to call the quill and the reed pen, with their element of self-will, the ideal artistic tools.

In the past, pen drawings were usually executed in ink which was made from oak-apples and vitriol, and which eventually turned brown; bistre, a brown solution of pine-soot in water, or a black wash made from lampblack or candleblack dissolved in gum-water, were also used. Sepia, which is a brown ink made from the colouring-matter of the cuttlefish, came into use in the eighteenth century.

The paper used is frequently tinted, the highlights in the drawing being picked out with white paint, or else it is covered with a light wash to give it a delicate tone. The colour of the wash must be carefully kept subordinate to the lines of the drawing, to prevent it destroying the draughtsmanlike quality of the penstrokes.

The characteristic appearance of a pen drawing is caused by the fact that all pens produce a relatively hard line. Pure line is the basic element, and although it may be considerably varied in width and serve for anything from quick impressionistic sketches to minutely calculated, highly finished drawings, from very subjective to very objective, realistic drawings, it cannot be used for soft tones and gradual transitions. Contrasts of light and shade are obtained with close or open hatching or by using several different nibs. Thus a pen drawing achieves its effect with the abstract element of line, not by changes of tone and even less by areas of flat colour. To a certain extent a true pen drawing should look as if it

Alfred Kubin (b. 1877): 'Promenade'. Pen drawing

were written, in the same way that the brush 'writes' in an Eastern painting. This is not only because its style is linear and because it lies flat on the picture plane, but—on another level—because it cannot produce an illusion of three dimensions like chalk or pastel. The individual line as it were de'scribes' with isolated strokes the essential characteristics of the forms; it abstracts, characterizes, suggests, or even exaggerates, but it does not create an illusion of reality.

'Abbreviated and summary, the drawing has in most cases retained an element of magic. It takes the contour as its starting-point and produces a kind of shorthand record of reality. It conjures up rather than creates an image.'[35] The flow and character of the lines assume an intrinsic value—if they do not originally possess it—almost beyond rational comprehension. These lines do much more than merely describe; they have an expressive and decorative existence of their own, a quality which may reach uncanny proportions, for instance, in the work of Alfred Kubin. A pen drawing, like handwriting, is the most direct possible means of expression. The artist's personality can find expression without the hindrance of complicated technical methods, 'flowing from the pen' in powerful, sweeping strokes or in clean, accurate lines and fine, delicate flicks. This is why a pen drawing often looks so fresh and spontaneous and why the artist can communicate his ideas in such a lively and direct way. Of any drawing instrument the pen, with its pure dynamic line, offers the artist the greatest scope for the expression of his individual genius.

194

THE WOODCUT IN EUROPE

MATERIALS: Block of wood (usually pear or alder). Proving ink. Watercolours for coloured woodcuts

TOOLS: Cutters and gouges, of various widths. Burnisher and dabber for hand printing

The woodcut is the oldest graphic medium which is reproduceable. It is a relief-printing technique, which means that the passages to be printed on the paper are left standing in the wood block, while the rest is cut away with gouges.

The origin of relief-printing is to be found in the wooden, metal, and stone dies used in antiquity. Printed textiles were made in the East in the early Middle Ages, but the earliest extant pictorial woodcuts date from around the end of the fourteenth century and probably came from Germany. In France and Holland woodcuts were also produced at an early date. Two factors favoured the growth of the woodcut; one was the introduction of paper into Europe, in the second half of the fourteenth century; the other, the basic reason for its development, was the growing practice of having private prayers, which created a demand for cheap substitutes for the costly paintings in the churches. This is why the earliest woodcuts were fairly large single sheets with representations of religious subjects. At first these were simple drawings without any kind of modelling, coloured by hand; but later the coloured illuminations were replaced by hatching on the woodcut itself. The woodcut

did not become an artistic medium of really high standing until 1460, mainly through the work of Michael Wohlgemut; then, particularly in Germany, it developed very quickly, reaching its peak in Dürer's day.

With the development of the decorative element in Renaissance art the woodcut was displaced by the line-engraving, which had technical possibilities of a different kind; now used no more for independent works of art, it became almost exclusively a medium for illustration until it was revived by Menzel, Rethel, and Doré in the nineteenth century. By

Ernst Ludwig Kirchner (1880–1938). 'Landscape in the Taunus'. Woodcut

the end of the century the invention of photography had brought objective representation to such perfection that artists reacted and found an outlet in a subjective form of expression; the woodcut was an especially suitable medium for this 'expressionistic' idiom and became widely used again.

For woodcutting, a wood block, usually pear or alder is used, the wood being cut along the grain. If the 'end-grain' is used, i.e. the wood is cut across the grain, this is called wood-engraving, a technique which was invented in about 1800. Pear and alder wood have the advantages of being of uniform density and toughness, and having the right hardness, as well as the greatest resistance to changes of moisture and temperature. The wood block must be absolutely dry, and its surface smooth and free of knots. The surface is given a thin chalk ground; the drawing is then traced on and cut out of the wood with cutters and gouges. 'The block cutter must think entirely in terms of his medium, not in terms of drawing. The design must grow out of the wood, it must emerge as he cuts.'[36] No other technique owes so much to its material; the grain, resistance and solidity of the wood should all be noticeable in the proof. The nature of the technique enforces a simple treatment, but this simplification can be a very valuable factor, as is borne out by Braque: 'The limitations imposed on the artist by his medium engender new forms, stimulate him to new creativeness and shape his style. Progress in art consists not in widening its boundaries, but in recognizing them better.'

198

Jost Amman: 'A Nobleman from Brunswick'. 1589.
Woodcut. This woodcut emulates the painterly and tonal effects of a line-engraving, partly
by the use of cross–hatching, which is intrinsically alien to the technique

The woodcut is not a good medium for a detailed and narrative style; this is the domain of the 'painterly' techniques. Its characteristic style is the cryptic, suggestive statement, and the emphasis of fundamental forms, which can be achieved with both linear and tonal techniques. The early masters mostly worked in the linear style, whereas modern artists prefer to exploit the contrasts between black and white, or black and coloured surfaces. Chiaroscuro woodcuts in particular should confine themselves to essentials. (In the Middle Ages, when the woodcut technique was mainly linear, coloured woodcuts were rare.) In the seventeenth and eighteenth centuries the special properties of the wood came to be ignored to the detriment of the technique, and the woodcut was used to imitate line-engraving, i.e. to obtain 'painterly' and naturalistic effects; this was done partly through the cutting technique and partly by the use of several blocks for the same print, each block representing a different tone of the same basic colour. The artistic level of the woodcut deteriorated as a result; its own expressive language was handicapped, but it could not compete with that of the line-engraving.

The examples of medieval and modern woodcuts reproduced here are both true to the medium and therefore of high artistic merit; on the other hand, the late sixteenth-century work, 'A Nobleman from Brunswick', shows a contradiction between material and technique, resulting in a lack of unity.

THE JAPANESE COLOUR PRINT

MATERIALS:	Block of cherry wood. Soft, absorbent, and usually ivory-coloured paper
TOOLS:	Cutters
PRINTING MATERIAL:	Water-bound colours (until the nineteenth century mostly obtained from plants)

When we speak of the Japanese woodcut, we usually mean the fully developed colour print which was invented in the 1760's and reached its full development within about twenty years of that date.

The simple black-and-white print had already existed for a thousand years, the oldest dated woodcuts being from the year A.D. 740. But until well into the seventeenth century the woodcut was no more than a method of reproducing paintings. Only after the unification of Japan and the subsequent period of peace, when the bourgeois class became wealthy and eager for culture, did the woodcut become an independent means of expression. The chief instrument of this change was Moronobu, who was born around the year 1638 and died in 1694. The works of the famous painters were only within the reach of the wealthy, but the colour print, which, unlike a painting was not unique, offered the mass of the people a very good substitute.

At first ordinary woodcuts were coloured by hand or with a stencil. The development of the colour print proper, that is, a woodcut made with several colour blocks, began in the middle of the eighteenth century. This new colour print now became an independent art form, as opposed to its Chinese counterpart, which remained a technique for reproducing well-known paintings. The most important artist of this period was Haronobu (1725–70).

W. Boller[37] wrote the following about the technique of colour printing: 'The Japanese artist does not (therefore) design a complete picture but makes several individual pictures, each in a single colour, which are sent individually to the cutter's workshop to be completed. Each block, i.e. each colour, has its own picture; the block-cutter pastes this picture on to the wood, cuts away all the white parts and leaves the coloured parts standing, thereby obtaining the printing block. A picture which has twenty different colours thus requires twenty blocks, and the artist must design twenty different monochrome pictures. The picture can only be brought into being when the printer has all the blocks; and until all the component parts are brought together neither the block-cutter nor the printer can anticipate what the picture will look like. Even the artist only sees his picture for the first time when it comes from the printer. . . . The incredibly complicated process of colour printing allows such extremely refined colouring that, for various reasons, its technical possibilities are far wider than any brush technique. Let us only mention the process of relief-printing, i.e.

pressing the paper out into relief, so that the picture is produced by the shadows thrown by the depressions. The colours can be printed into the depressed areas of the paper, or the paper can be brought into relief after the colours have been printed by impressing it.' New tones may be obtained by printing one colour over another, and the effect can be varied by applying the colour in different consistencies, or by wiping it on the block.

But a complicated and versatile technique does not in itself constitute an art, particularly one that is so representative of a whole people—not only of an individual artist—as the Japanese colour print. The latent artistic potentialities of colour printing were brought out in a unique way, and were made possible because the characteristic elements of the wood-cutting technique found their counterpart in the Japanese philosophy of life. Thus a very individual artistic inclination created for itself a suitable means of expression and then perfected it.

The elements of the colour print are line and pure flat colour. As a technique it is hardly suitable for giving an illusion of three dimensions, or achieving modulations of colour or 'painterly' effects. So the character of the technique is not conducive to a faithful representation of nature with all the subjective and transitory elements of perspective and light and shade, but to a symbolism expressed in a flat pattern, to an abstract imagery created with line and flat tone. This quality fully reflects the Japanese vision, which is characterized by clarity, firmness and powerful concentration. 'It is possible to see at a glance that the Japanese attitude to the woodcut as well as to painting is fundamentally different from the Chinese; the emphasis is on the sharp, polished form, on capturing the essence of things, hardly on spiritualization; it is more suggestive in its means of expression, more linear, much more carefully constructed. One cannot sum all this up in the word "realistic". The heart of the matter is that the individual line in a Japanese woodcut appears more charged with meaning, and the whole composition is firmly knit together, whereas in Chinese art everything hangs together freely and loosely. The Chinese hums his melody of the infinity of nature softly to himself, but the Japanese sings out with a clear voice into the laughing world his song of the joys of being alive.'

This precision and compactness found its ideal expression in the woodcut. The technique of line and flat tone was a perfect medium for translating the Japanese conception of life into visual form, with its expressive contours, well-balanced areas of light and dark, and skilful distribution and grouping of colour. Emil Praetorius has called these colour prints 'brilliant collector's pieces of graphic art, masterly in their elegance of line, their forceful language of contrasts and skilfully divided planes, and the product of the clearest artistic understanding'.

It is impossible to have any real idea of the attractiveness of these works without seeing the originals, for apart from the line and the colour, the impressions made on the paper in the printing play an important part; even so, our reproduction shows a little of the

Hiroshige (1797–1858): 'The Rain-bridge'. Colour print

fascination of the colour print. How stimulating an art form can be when purpose and technique are ideally matched is demonstrated by the influence of the Japanese colour print on European painting since Manet; while the development of the modern poster would have been unthinkable without the Japanese influence.

MATERIALS: Copper-plate printing ink. Polished copper plate

TOOLS: Burin, scraper, burnisher, roulette

After the woodcut the line-engraving is the oldest graphic process; but whereas the wood-cut prints in relief, line-engraving is an intaglio process, i.e. the drawing is engraved into the copper and then inked in, so that when an impression is made, the engraved line yields the ink. The copper plate should be about one-tenth of an inch thick, and of uniform hardness. The surface is polished and often grounded with chalk, and the drawing, or at least the contours, are traced on to the ground. The lines are then engraved into the copper with a burin, a chisel-like steel tool with a sharp point.

The burin must be pushed forward to overcome the resistance of the metal so that the hand cannot move as freely as if it were handling a pen. Since the burin can only move in one direction, curved lines are made by rotating the plate, for which purpose it rests on a round, leather-covered cushion. The character of the engraved line is determined by the resistance of the metal, because this resistance forces the lines into a severe and more or less parallel formation. An engraving of a pure style will retain this linear character even if fine parallel- or cross-hatching is used for representing graduated tones. Although wood-cutting was also a purely linear technique in its early stages, the engraved line is much finer and can be used for much more subtle transitions, if only because a line in a woodcut has to be made by cutting two grooves and leaving a ridge between them (which means that it cannot possibly be really fine or line-like), whereas the engraved line is a pictorial element in itself.

Whereas in Italy a constant and close connection with painting gave it a certain monumentality, in Germany engraving profited from being a branch of the goldsmith's craft; north of the Alps it therefore evolved a style of its own and a technical superiority which gave it greater scope for development. Lines became more energetic, the modulations richer, so that it was possible to obtain more solidity and greater depth of tone. The highest achievements of the engraver's art are the works of the school of Rubens, which reproduced and made known the great Flemish artist's paintings, and of a number of artists at the court of Louis XIV.

If the technique is too perfectly mastered there is a danger that the engraving will become smooth and degenerate into mere slickness. Before long the less limited techniques of etching and aquatint were to develop from line-engraving, and from the eighteenth century onwards it was used almost exclusively for reproduction. It is almost obsolete today.

Albrecht Dürer: 'St Jerome in his study' (detail). 1514. Line-engraving

| MATERIALS: | Copper plate with acid-proof resinous ground. Dilute nitric acid (mordant). Engraving ink |
| TOOLS: | Etching needles (steel points of various sizes) |

Etching was invented at the beginning of the sixteenth century. The materials used are similar to line-engraving but the technique and therefore the expressive possibilities of etching are very different. While the engraver must laboriously dig his burin into the copper the etcher draws on the thin film of resinous ground almost as effortlessly as if it were paper. In this way he exposes the copper so that when the plate is covered with acid it penetrates into the exposed areas and etches the drawing into the metal.

A strictly linear treatment as in line-engraving is not necessary with etching, as it is the ground and not the metal which is incised. The etcher is free to draw in large, sweeping strokes; he can record his ideas spontaneously, yet they can immediately be reproduced. Etching presents hardly any technical difficulties whereas the handling of the burin demands considerable skill, and it is because of the simplicity of the etching technique that it has always been the favourite means of reproduction with painters, sculptors, and draughtsmen.

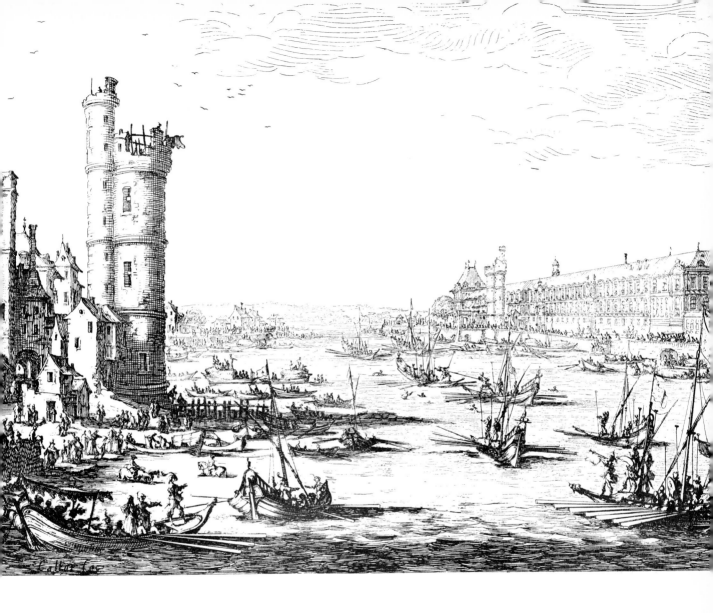

Jacques Callot (1592–1635): 'View of the Louvre' (detail). Etching

Once fully developed, etching offered yet another possibility. The process of 'stopping-out' made it possible to obtain a great variety of tones and lines. If the plate is exposed to acid only for a short time the lines are but delicately etched in so that they hold only a very small amount of ink. The areas to be printed in this way, for instance, landscape backgrounds, are protected or stopped out with shellac or wax and the plate is then treated with acid again; the unprotected areas will be more strongly etched and make a darker impression. If this admittedly complex process is repeated it is possible to obtain rich gradations and atmospheric effects which are out of the range of almost all other techniques.

The possibilities of etching were not fully exploited for a long time. In Dürer's day the plates were made of iron because acids which would etch copper were unknown, but even after the substitution of copper the linear technique was still adhered to and it was a hundred years before the stopping-out process was invented. The first to explore all the possibilities of this technique systematically was Jacques Callot.[33] Callot'[5] etchings contained hundreds of tiny figures accurately represented in space and atmosphere, and were greatly admired. He perfected a method of aerial perspective and accurate spatial transitions which it would have been impossible to obtain in a purely linear technique.

The greatest name in etching is without doubt Rembrandt. Technically Rembrandt surpassed Callot because he was the first to use the so-called dry-point technique.[39] By dry-point is understood the process of engraving without etching, i.e. drawing with a dry

Rembrandt (1606–69): 'Christ teaching'. Etching and dry-point

point or needle on the bare copper plate. A line engraved in this way leaves a small ridge or burr on either side of it, whereas in line-engraving the metal shavings are dug right out. Although a dry-point line is necessarily thin and delicate, the burr takes the colour well and gives the dry-point a rich, velvety texture. Rembrandt found this technique very useful for chiaroscuro. However, a dry-point cannot be reproduced indefinitely because the burr soon becomes depressed again with printing.

The plate on page 215 shows a dry-point by Max Beckmann, who made frequent use of this technique. It is a good illustration of the characteristic dark patches and the bloom of the dry-point line.

Max Beckmann
(1884–1950):
'Weeping woman'.
Dry-point

MATERIALS:	Copper plate. Engraving ink
TOOLS:	Cradle, scraper, burnisher, roulette

Engraving was used almost from the time it was invented as a means of reproducing famous paintings and making them known to a wider public. But neither line-engraving proper nor etching was ideally suited for reproducing oil paintings, because both techniques worked essentially with line, whereas a painting is built up with graduated tones. In the words of Singer: 'A linear technique is out of the question for colour printing. Attempts to use it have shown that this is not only technically almost impossible, but an artistic paradox. The white paper shows between the lines and naturally affects their tone value; it disperses and distorts the coloured lines and destroys the colour effect. Colour printing is only feasible in a technique which employs flat tones.'

From the line-engraving to the colour print was still a far cry; the next step was to find a technique which would print flat tones in black and white. The earliest of these techniques was mezzotint engraving which was invented in Germany in 1642. The principle under-lying mezzotint is the uniform roughening of the whole plate by means of a so-called

Petrus Schenk (1660–1718):
Portrait of M. van Rhede.
Mezzotint

cradle or rocker, a knife with a curved serrated edge. An impression of this surface would be absolutely black. Working from dark to light, the grain is removed from the areas which are to appear light with a scraper and burnisher. The more this rough surface is planed away the less ink it holds, and there is no limit to the tones which may be obtained in this way. The fact that the surface of the plate must be of a uniform texture, which involves going over it again and again in all conceivable directions, makes the process of pricking a very tedious affair, but the scraping and smoothing of the plate afterwards is quite simple.

From the beginning the mezzotint was almost exclusively used for reproducing paintings and it has now been completely replaced by modern colour photogravure and photography. The reason it never reached the status of an art in its own right is that it did not

Charles Knight (1743–1826):
Portrait of Lady Manners.
Colour print

attempt to do more than to imitate oil painting, so that it had no particular expressive qualities of its own. The best mezzotints, however, have a 'painterly' quality unsurpassed in any other process of black-and-white reproduction.

The best coloured reproductions of paintings were also produced with the help of the mezzotint, in a technique called colour printing. The first attempts to print several coloured copper plates one on top of the other date from as early as around 1600; but prints as delightful as the portrait of Lady Manners by Charles Knight, illustrated here, were only made possible by combining mezzotint with the principle of multiple colour printing, in some cases as many as eight differently coloured plates being used. The best colour prints were produced in the eighteenth century by English artists; these are now extremely costly and much sought after.

AQUATINT ENGRAVING

MATERIALS:	Polished copper plate. Powdered asphaltum or resin. Shellac or asphalt varnish. Engravers' ink
TOOLS:	Needle. Brush for application of stopping-out varnish

Aquatint, like mezzotint, is an extension of line-engraving, to enable it to print areas of tone. The aquatint technique was invented in the eighteenth century by the French artist Jean Baptiste Leprince, and is practised in the following way.

First of all the drawing is transferred in outline on to the plate, which is then sprinkled with a uniform layer of asphaltum or resin powder. The plate is heated enough to make the grains of the powder adhere to it but not so much that they melt or coalesce. In this way the plate is covered with a fine granular surface which resists the action of the mordant, so that it can only bite into the minute interstices. An aquatint proof examined under a magnifying glass shows very small white dots on a dark ground. Resin has a lower melting-point than asphaltum and is used if a finer grain is required, while asphaltum is used for a coarser one.

When the plate has been prepared in this way, the parts which are to be absolutely white are brushed over with stopping-out varnish or asphalt varnish. The plate is then covered

Picasso: 'Head of a goat'. 1952. Sugar aquatint

with mordant, which of course can only bite into the intervals between the particles and leaves the grains themselves and the stopped-out areas intact. The portions attacked by the acid are etched, and print as a dark tone. This process is repeated for each tone required, several tones being obtainable in this way. But each tone is uniform and ends in an abrupt contour and there are no gentle gradations as in mezzotint. The aquatint therefore owes its character to the combination of etched lines and the clearly differentiated tones produced by the stopping-out technique.

The master of aquatint engraving was Goya, who hardly ever used more than two or three tones. The print by him reproduced here clearly shows the difference between aquatint and mezzotint. In the one the tones are distinctly marked off from each other; the other has gentle gradations which closely resemble the most 'painterly' of paintings (see p. 217).

It is not surprising that aquatint, the more difficult of the two techniques, should be popular again today, when even painting aims to be flat. It is used particularly by the artists of the French school; Picasso, Miró, and Rouault all worked in aquatint. They used a technique called sugar aquatint, in which the drawing, instead of being engraved into the metal, is applied to a clean plate with a black gouache dissolved in sugar-water. The whole plate is then grounded, put in water and rubbed lightly with a soft cloth to remove the ground from the drawn or painted portions. The process is now continued as in ordinary aquatint, i.e. the plate is sprinkled with asphaltum or resin powder, etched and stopped out.

MATERIALS: Lithography stone (fine-grained, porous limestone). Lithographic chalk, lithographic ink, asphaltum. Printing ink

TOOLS: Brushes for applying lithographic ink; scraper, needle, lithography pen

Lithography is a surface-printing process which was invented by Aloys Senefelder at the end of the eighteenth century. The most important name in lithography is that of Honoré Daumier (1808–79), whose satirical black-and-white lithographs were published by the thousand in the nineteenth century. Some of these appeared as separate sheets, but most of them were printed in periodicals; Max Slevogt greatly extended the scope of lithography as a book illustration technique to a hitherto unknown degree. Toulouse-Lautrec was the pioneer of colour lithography; he raised it once and for all to the status of a fine art and its use is still spreading today.

A lithograph is made in the following way. The design is drawn on the stone in reverse with lithography chalk or ink; the stone, being somewhat porous, absorbs both grease and water. The stone is then 'etched' with a solution of gum-arabic containing a little nitric acid, moistened and inked in with a hand-roller. The ink only adheres to the portions of the stone which have been drawn on, and the proofs can now be pulled. Several stones are required for a coloured lithograph.

Ever since Senefelder's time attempts have been made to substitute metal plates for the heavy and expensive stone, especially for large lithographs. Today zinc plates are used for preference; aluminium plates are less common. Picasso used zinc plates almost exclusively. The drawing and printing procedure is the same for a metal plate as for stone, except that phosphoric acid is used instead of nitric acid.

It is possible to avoid drawing on the stone in reverse by making the design on lithographic paper, from which it is transferred on to the stone or plate.

Although lithography was originally developed as a purely reproductive process, it now takes its place as an independent art form. There is indeed no reason why lithography should be purely mechanical. In the first place the artist can draw freely and spontaneously on the stone without encountering technical difficulties, and in the second place the colour can be applied in such a way that each proof, especially in colour lithography, can be unique; in any case, there is always a slight variation from one proof to the next.

Compared with, say, woodcutting or line-engraving, lithography leaves the artist a great deal of freedom. He can use line, tone, half-tone and colour, and he can work with white on black, as Picasso, for example, often does. Consequently a lithograph does not

Richard P. Bonington: 'La rue du gros Horloge , Rouen,' 1824. Lithograph

have the unmistakable personality of works in other techniques—in fact some lithographs might almost be mistaken for chalk or charcoal drawings. It is perhaps true to say that lithography has fewer specific expressive potentialities than the more limited graphic processes.

Monotype is related to lithography because it is also a surface-printing technique. A monotype is made by drawing first on any kind of plate, let us say a sheet of glass; the plate, however, is not 'etched' in any way. The pull is then made with damp paper; naturally only a single pull can be taken. Since the colour is absorbed by the paper it is possible to obtain very attractive effects with monotype which are somewhat related to watercolour. It is an interesting technique, but necessarily limited in scope. The Expressionists employed it occasionally and a few artists still use it today.

Karl Rödel (b. 1907):
'Zebu'.
Five-colour lithograph.
Pull of first two colours

Pull of first three colours

Pull of first four colours

The completed five-colour lithograph

III   APPENDIX

Apart from questions of space, there is, in fact, no need to follow up in detail the technical development of every single work of art. It is quite sufficient to study a few examples carefully. This will be done here by speculating on the possible uses for particular tools, materials and supports on the one hand, and on the other by pointing out the part played by each of these elements in pictures already existing. In the plan to be followed here the tools are discussed first.

How the Tools influence the Support and the Materials

To use a watercolour brush with its soft, pliant head demands experience, a steady hand and a light touch. With this tool more than any other the skill and sensitive touch of the artist is of supreme importance.

It is not surprising that the peoples of the Far East, with their extraordinary skill and sensitivity, became masters of this art. Does not one of their poets say that 'The mighty tree is felled by the storm, but the supple reed withstands it. Though the rock is of hard stone, it is finally destroyed by the soft water.' The peoples who had this attitude to life used the soft expressive brush as a writing instrument.

Chinese and Japanese writing characters must be drawn extremely accurately, yet they leave room for an individual style and a variety of pictorial combinations which would be quite impossible with our alphabet. The Far Eastern people begin to use brushes at a very

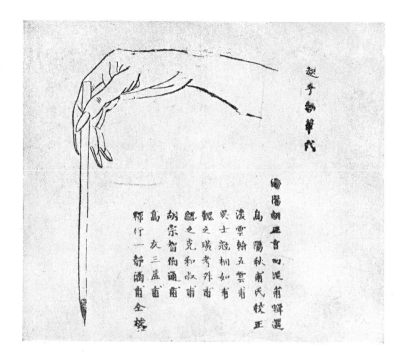

Japanese woodcut,
showing method of
holding the brush

early age, so that finally they are virtuosi in the art of calligraphy. The syllabic symbols were originally pictographs, but they have become so simplified and stereotyped that it is often impossible for anyone but an expert to recognize the original forms. Individual ways of forming the characters were only made possible by the development of personal styles of brushwork. The brush is controlled from the shoulder-joint, not, as in Europe, from the wrist. The shape of the letter follows the brush stroke, beginning in a sharp point and turning into a broad, straight (or curved) wedge—or vice versa. These brushes hold a great deal of paint, which makes it possible to draw the characters in long, continuous

Japanese picture roll.
Brush drawing on silk-paper.
The paint is used in various
consistencies, e.g. very liquid
for the drop-like dots, dry for
the horse's mane. The position
in which the brush is held may
be inferred from the flow of
the line

strokes, and the interruptions necessary for refilling are avoided. This means that the artist must never hesitate. Techniques like encaustic, and even mosaic, seem very cumbersome by comparison, because every step forward entails complicated technical processes, and every break fresh deliberation. But the brush and watercolour technique is bold and sweeping and this is why the watercolour brush is better than other tools for bringing out subconscious creative powers, and, like handwriting, it is especially responsive to a spirited temperament. The brush is dynamic, to a certain extent, like the watercolour with which it is used. The tension and movement in the figures of the Palaeolithic cave paintings of eastern Spain show how ideal an instrument it is for capturing momentary impressions; it is used to the same effect in the fleeting sketches on stone (*ostraca*) at El Amarna, as well as in certain landscapes and erotic scenes at Pompeii. Only the watercolour brush makes it possible to produce inspired sketches and improvizations—which nevertheless look so effortless, as if they had been written—like the bamboo leaves on page 243. The paper on which the Chinese and Japanese write is thin and absorbent, so that each brush stroke is immediately absorbed on contact. On denser paper the effect is quite different; the paint remains in drops on the surface, and the water evaporates, though it may eventually run a little of its own accord. The flow of the paint is thus determined by the brush stroke as well as by the paint spreading afterwards.

A rough ground produces quite a different effect from a smooth one: the brush strokes become rougher too, and their edges are less definite. It therefore requires different expressive means, such as tone and colour contrasts, which are characteristics of Impressionism. This explains why the Impressionists used textured, beaten paper for their lively watercolours of boulevard scenes and landscapes. Even the Oriental brush paintings show that the tone contrasts are achieved largely through changes in speed and pressure, not only through the diminishing flow of paint. On a rough-grained paper these phenomena become decisive pictorial elements: if a fairly dry brush is drawn very quickly over a sheet of

238

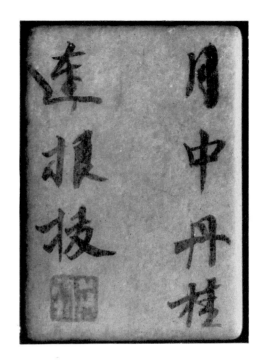

Chinese characters on the reverse of a stone writing-tablet; the manipulation of the brush-tip may be detected

rough-grained paper the paint adheres only to the raised parts, while the depressed parts retain their original colour.

A different kind of paint, body colour mixed with white, for instance, again changes the character of the picture. Being thicker, it can be more evenly applied and also dries more evenly. No surprises are to be expected with a pointed brush loaded with body colour. It does not matter very much whether the paint is applied fast or slowly. However, there is less similarity than one might suppose between this method and painting on an absorbent ground with thin transparent paint; the difference is indeed fundamental. A stroke painted with the latter cannot be worked over or corrected. The paper forms a uniform substructure and plays a decisive part, whereas opaque body colour eliminates the paper altogether and creates an entirely new surface. On the other hand, a fairly dry brush passed lightly over rough-grained paper deposits paint only on the protuberances. Body colour flows more quickly than thin wash on account of its greater power of cohesion, so that a given amount will cover only a fraction of the surface covered by the same amount of wash. This is an important consideration, because it affects the size of the picture to be painted in such a medium. Wash and watercolour impose certain limitations of size, but body colour leads to a miniature technique. In medieval miniatures, scale and technique are in perfect harmony, especially in the famous Islamic miniatures which were also the foundation of Indian and Persian lacquer painting, and the result is a degree of perfection rarely achieved elsewhere.

Brushes made of hair can also be used with thicker paint. Sign-writers use them—with oil paint—for lining and contours; in oil painting they are also indispensable for line-work and detail. They are exclusively used in decorating pottery, in glass painting and, particularly, in peasant art, because they have the advantage that they can be used for drawing as well as filling in, in addition to lining and writing.

They are also largely used in oil or tempera for paintings where the paint is built up in thin successive layers. The smooth, enamel-like paint surface and the limited scale characteristic of such pictures allows them to be painted with somewhat the same method as a miniature. The simple 'colouring-in' technique should also be mentioned here; this is familiar to all of us from our earliest painting efforts, and has always been one of the principal uses of the watercolour brush. It is a technique which is practised by the majority of primitive peoples and is to be found in the murals and papyri of ancient Egypt, in early medieval illuminations, in Chinese and Japanese woodcuts and elsewhere.

Although this list is by no means exhaustive, only one more example will be mentioned

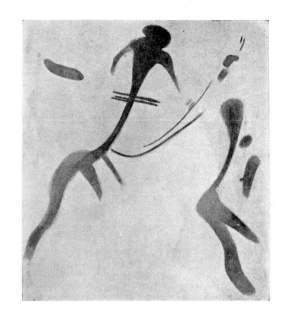

Two archers, Valltorta cave, E. Spain. Each about 8 in. high. Painted on rock. According to the experiments of Professor Obermaier and the author, brush-like tools were used and the paint was applied in liquid form in a glazing technique, usually in two layers

as an increasingly important application of the watercolour brush. This is fresco painting. The painting ground in a fresco consists of a very delicate, thin layer of lime. The soft brush drags the watery paint through the tacky surface, picking up some particles and losing others. To paint across lines made in this way is almost impossible, and even more so to lay another coat on top of them or make alterations. Every line is immediately absorbed and permanently preserved in the ground, and is thus quite indelible. This process alone shows how unique is the fresco technique, and that it cannot be compared with either watercolour or opaque techniques. The surface of a fresco is composed of hatchings, as is clearly seen in the two early Renaissance heads reproduced on page 245.

This linear structure recurs elsewhere: is it not reminiscent of the paintings of van Gogh, of oil paint, canvas, and bristle brushes?

A paint brush made of bristles is firmer than one which is made of hair and produces a surer and more precise stroke, the same width from beginning to end. Being less sensitive to the hand's changing pressure, it carries out the artist's intention fairly accurately. On the other hand it is coarser as an instrument. The shorter the bristles, the more firm is the brush, but the less paint it holds. The width of the brush stroke is in direct relation to the width and length of the head, while its length depends either on the capacity of the bristles or the texture of the ground. In the case of thick paint, a bristle brush is more than a mere carrier; it gives each individual stroke its final form, and often leaves an impression of the bristles on it. This is a particularly marked instance of a tool moulding the paint, and consequently the whole picture, and regarded in this light van Gogh's paintings 'spring from the technique' in a magnificent way.

Van Gogh's manner is not far different from that of the Pointillists (Seurat and Signac). Pointillism, a descendant of Impressionism, flourished at the turn of the century; a Pointillist painting was built up of small dots of colour which only became intelligible when added up collectively in the spectator's eye. A thin, round bristle brush was the tool used for this technique and the paint was applied very thickly, as it was in all the methods described above.

It is of course possible to use a bristle brush for laying down broad, uniform passages of paint. In fact, in the case of water-bound body colour, a bristle brush is better for this purpose than one made of hair: it spreads the slow-drying paint very simply without leaving brush marks, and there is no danger that the colour will be lifted off or smudged when overpainted. All medieval tempera painting, as well as the later tempera and oil techniques, are built up on this technical foundation. The separate parts of the picture could be smoothly and evenly painted with local colour, the gaily coloured pictures produced in this way

Detail from a Chinese paper screen.
The bamboo leaves are painted with wedge-shaped downward brush
strokes. This method, originating in a free-hand technique, cannot be
copied like a Renaissance painting painted in several layers, since the
'handwriting' depends largely on nuances which are unique

243

revealing a primitive delight in smooth surfaces. Modern painting shows a similar liking for flat colour without transitions or contours which is to be seen, for instance, in the work of Carl Grossberg, who brought this technique to mature perfection.

The ability of the bristle brush to graduate thick oil colour is well known, and the broader the brush, the grander is the effect achieved. But a painting knife is even better for this purpose: with it the thick paint can be squeezed into shape and given a visible edge, rather in the same way that the plaster is trowelled on to house walls in southern Germany. The ground can be completely covered, or the thickness of the paint varied by altering the pressure of the hand or laid on quite lightly so that it only covers the ground in parts and looks almost transparent. The difference in technique between painting thick, creamy oil paint and quick-drying, lean tempera with a painting knife is very great.

It is important to note that a bristle brush can also be used with thinner paint. Only a single but very impressive example is shown (p. 247): it is a Chinese writing character (meaning 'long life'), painted in three bold strokes on a piece of felt paper laid on a mat, with what appears to be an extremely broad bristle brush, but is in fact a split bamboo stick. The 'brush' has been lightly dipped in paint and drawn over the surface, so that the application is rather dry. Added to this is the effect produced by the wickerwork mat, which is rather like that of the rough surface of beaten paper mentioned above. The paint has been deposited only where the protuberances in the mat press the paper up; it is the same technique that children use to make a pencil rubbing of a coin on a sheet of paper.

The uses of the bristle brush bring us to the quill, reed and steel pen, and to the engraving tools used by primitive peoples for incising drawings and decorating pottery; the slate pencil of the schoolboy is also used in a similar way. With all these tools drawing a line is more laborious, and sweeping curves are awkward to make. The hand has to struggle against the resistance. But in this harshness and inflexibility of the elements of the technique lies a particular charm—there is, for instance, scarcely anyone who does not like etchings.

The technique of fresco painting.
Details of Renaissance frescoes

Above: detail showing marks made by liner on the tacky plaster surface

Below: detail showing drawing made with tip of brush on surface of plaster which has already begun to set

This is also the place to mention the gouge used for woodcutting. Burying itself in the hard wood, it resists the rounding and modelling movement of the hand even more strongly. The singularly taut curves of a woodcut have been compared with some truth to a drawn bow. This quality gives the woodcuts of the East, particularly of Japan, the dryness and severity, the magnificent classical composure, the formality and the monumentality so different from the delicate improvisations of the brush. It is quite unjust that laymen should speak of woodcuts being 'only prints'. It is the *original* that is valued; in this case, the original drawing. This distinction mainly applies to European woodcuts, which were mostly only pen drawings transferred on to a wood block for reproduction purposes, in which process all the elements of the technique were usually much abused. No such prejudice attaches to the true woodcut, which is in quite a different category, and anyone who refuses to hang a good print deprives himself of the enjoyment of an art form which is unique.

In woodcutting the original is cut into the block of wood and what we see is only an impression in reverse. But in one form of the technique we see the original: this is Chinese Coromandel work, justly one of the most famous techniques of all. Here the wood base is given a good coat of chalk and, when dry, is covered with lacquer. The design is then cut out of the lacquer down to the depth of the chalk, the contours being left standing as black relief lines. The exposed chalk is painted in with plant and mineral colours. The technique is identical with woodcutting, as is the style; as in a colour print or hand-coloured woodcut, the sections which have been cut away are coloured in. But however carefully a woodcut is printed, it cannot convey the spontaneous quality of the cutting technique in anything like the same way as a Coromandel screen, where the areas of lacquer left after the cutting are magically intertwined with the shiny ridges and form a delicate harmony with the rich, matt colours.

From here it is only a single step to stencilling. A stencil, like a colour print, consists of

Chinese character, on a scroll.
The felt-paper has been laid on a mat,
whose texture is rubbed through into
the design

Incised drawing on ivory.
Stone Age
The precise, regular lines are drawn with
a flint tool

a combination of several individual coloured surfaces. It can also be enriched by spraying, a technique of equally ancient origin, as may be seen in the sprayed outline drawings of hands found in the caves of the Stone Age. Today spraying is done with sieves, spray-guns, and vaporizers, and although the variety of colour obtainable in this way is limited, it produces subtler gradations than any other technique.

How the Support or the Ground influences the Materials and the Tools

If the support, or ground, consists of some unusual material, or even if it only has a particular texture, the character of a picture is strongly influenced by it. A medium-grained fresco ground, for instance, is obtrusive enough to make a realistic style of painting impossible. It is a well-known fact that to paint flesh convincingly on a plaster ground is almost impossible, however carefully it is done. This is why in fresco painting the forms must be stylized; the limited colour range and the white plaster showing through the paint make for a flat style.

The structure of brick, masonry and stone, strongly defined, clearly visible, have a similar influence on the painting ground. Their texture is so powerful that it shows through every sort of painting. The grain of wood appears as a linear texture.

In a glass painting the sheet of glass forms a barrier which the eye must first penetrate, and produces a sense of uncertainty as to the exact position of the picture plane. In addition there is a barely perceptible reflection of the picture in the form of a duplication of the contours, while at the same time the glass reflects its external surroundings. All this produces the same aggravating effect experienced by looking into a lake or a fountain, when the first impression is of a simultaneous image of the surface, a fish, possibly swimming along the ground at the bottom, and the reflection.

In the case of pottery the influence of the body, whether it consists of earthenware, stoneware, or porcelain, is so strong, both as a support and material, that great care must be taken to prevent the painted decoration from conflicting with it.

A support is noticeable not only by virtue of the material of which it consists, but by the influence which it exerts on the paint and its method of application. For instance, we all know the difference between writing on smooth and on textured paper. A pencil-line drawn on smooth paper is precise, on rough drawing paper it is ill-defined and scraggy.

249

A line drawn with red chalk or charcoal on a uniformly textured drawing paper is broken up into vertical parallel hatchings. Smooth paper is therefore the best for precise lines, textured paper for soft transitions. The artist of our Chinese character made an unusually rough surface for his drawing by laying a piece of thin felt paper on top of a coarse wicker mat; the application is therefore rough and coarse too.

The coarser the technique of the painting, the greater should be the distance between it and the spectator. Michelangelo used to roughen the surface of his plaster in order to make his frescoes look more monumental from a distance. In the caves of Altamira we find that certain parts of the very uneven rock have been worn smooth by sintering, while others, where no such process has occurred, are rough. The large animals (they are 3 to 7 feet high) are painted in rough and broken lines which make them look so naturalistic that several experts have been led to believe that the texture of fur was imitated intentionally. The only way of painting on such a rough surface was to dab the colour on in liquid form or rub it on with rough lumps. Several people have been tempted by the results of this enforced technique into making a comparison with modern impressionistic paintings.

But the smooth and even surfaces on which the rock paintings of eastern Spain were executed would not have taken this thick, pasty earth colour: the material used here was ink, and the corresponding tools, namely, brushes of hair. Consequently the figures are small, no more than about 4 to 8 inches high. The difference in style between these works and the Franco-Cantabrian paintings is less one of time and culture than of the surface on which they were executed.

Every surface or support, be it silk, canvas, hessian, or whatever, requires different tools and different consistencies of paint. A brush drawn quickly over a rough surface leaves paint only on the protuberances: the slower it is moved across the surface, the deeper the paint settles. The densest application possible on a rough ground is by 'stippling', or putting on the paint in adjacent dots, which produces a closely detailed execution. The dots

Rubbing of various textures, e.g. wood;
graphite pencil on paper

can also be placed at larger intervals and the combination of painted and unpainted surface produces the beautiful effect which is to be found in the paintings of Cézanne and van Gogh.

In techniques where watery paint is used, the density of the surface is of great importance. It determines how fast and how much the paint is absorbed; unsized paper, for instance, absorbs wet paint immediately and, once laid on, each dab of colour becomes the indelible imprint of the tool. An unprepared gesso ground acts in the same way: the paint sinks in immediately. Since it cannot run, wet paint in an absorbent surface therefore enforces a linear style: the lines dry immediately and stand out clearly against the light ground: their form and expression is final. Almost all Chinese and Japanese brush drawings depend on this, and so does under-glaze pottery decoration, though here the colour is often applied with a pen instead of a brush. For clear defined outlines, the second layer is not put on until the first is dry, as in watercolour or any paintings built up in layers, whereas a blurred and 'atmospheric' picture is obtained by an *al prima* method, i.e. by painting into the wet colour.

How the Materials influence the Tools and the Support

This brings us to the painting materials. In the case of a thin glaze the material is completely subjugated to the surface it is painted on, so that the final result is a combined effect of both elements. It does not matter whether the support is unprimed stone, masonry, earthenware, plaster, wood or paper, or whether it consists of some 'neutral' substance with an opaque ground: whatever it is, it invariably shimmers through the transparent paint; it remains the surface of the picture whatever happens. Watercolour is transparent and the charm of the watercolour technique depends, rather like fresco painting, on the combination of the glowing translucent colour and the white ground. In the case of fresco, this transparent effect is increased by the shimmering crystalline lime, and in a half-light a fresco glows in a most remarkable way. With the exception of black, which does not reflect light, almost all colours can be glazed or scumbled to give a translucent effect, or be glazed over with another colour.

After the thin glazes come the more viscous kinds of paints which, although they cover the painting surface like a light cloak, nevertheless leave its structure visible. A whitewashed brick wall or a piece of canvas covered with thick but fluid paint give the impression that the paint is bound directly to the support. A painting only becomes independent of its support if it can completely obliterate it, like impasto, grease paint, and enamel colours. In this case the painting surface is solely a support in the literal sense: it would not make any difference to the picture if it were lifted bodily off the support, whether it is of stone, wood, or metal—this is actually possible—and transferred to a different one.

Everyone is familiar with tempera and oil paint, but less so with wax paint, an even more independent medium, which was used so frequently in antiquity as 'make-up', both for the living and for wooden and stone statues. From this practice eventually developed the technique of painting on panels with hot wax, i.e. encaustic. The wooden panel was a completely 'neutral' surface and an encaustic painting could be executed on any other surface provided it was dry, even on glass. Some encaustic portraits are so uncannily life-like that they might almost have been modelled in the round, and although it may seem a little bold to compare them with the models in shop windows, with wax cabinets or the wax portraits of the nineteenth century, the affinity cannot be denied. Nevertheless, life-like though these wax figures may be, they are not in the least alive. If we tried to 'make up' a life-size portrait bust or full-length nude statue, we should discover that the truer to nature it is, the more lifeless. A faithful copy has a rigidity which eludes those very qualities which impart life—movement, breath, and the flicker of eyelashes—and the logical consequence of naturalism is nothing but an apparition.

The author's interest in old methods of mural painting, some of which are out of use today, led to a scheme to paint a cycle of murals for an office building using both old and modern techniques with the aim of providing a means of comparison. These paintings offered an opportunity of testing historical techniques in practice and, in the instance of Pompeian wall painting, of studying various problems connected with grounds and methods of execution.

This short account contains some fundamental reflections on the nature of mural painting, as well as on the individual techniques.

ENCAUSTIC

The main source for our knowledge of encaustic are the late Egyptian Faiyum portraits. Apart from two panel paintings whose authenticity is in dispute, 'Cleopatra with the Asp' and the so-called 'Muse of Cordona', they are the only remaining evidence of this ancient technique. With the help of one of these mummy portraits which forms part of our study collection, we hope to have gained some kind of insight into the encaustic technique.

It has to be remembered that the ancients did not know of sugar, and relied exclusively on honey for sweetening their foodstuffs. As a result, bee-keeping was far more widespread than it is today, and wax, the by-product of honey, was available in large quantities. This explains why wax played such an important role in antiquity and was used for very many purposes.

There is an ambiguous passage in Pliny which leaves us in doubt as to whether the Greeks and Romans used wax paint for their temple façades in a warm, liquid state, i.e. encaustic, or as a cold, liquid wax emulsion. The passage runs as follows:

'In ancient times there were (only) two methods of encaustic painting with wax and on ivory with the cestrum, until it became the custom to paint ships of war. Then the third method was added, that of melting the wax colours, and laying them on with a brush. This kind of painting applied to ships is proof against sun, wind and salt water.'[40]

What is certain is that melted, purified hard wax, the so-called 'punic wax', was used. According to Pliny and Dioscurides, the wax acquired extraordinary properties when melted several times in sea-water and combined with soda, in which process it also became bleached. It is possible that the hotter temperatures of the southern countries, i.e. Egypt, had an additional beneficial effect.

The tools found in the graves of painters at St-Herne-Hubert and St Médard-des-Prés raised further queries. These tools included a cauterium—a small spoon with a handle—which was also used for the mummy portraits, as well as a brush and a cestrum, a handled instrument like a stylus which was only used for wax painting on ivory. The existence of wax on ancient Egyptian reliefs has been proved. The Greeks used wax or wax paint for coating pictures as well as stone, wood (in the early days), and the porous stucco work on temples.

Finally there is the so-called *Ganosis*, used both by the Greeks and the Romans, for knowledge of which we are indebted to Vitruvius. This was a kind of varnish used for covering paintwork and marble statues endangered by exposure.

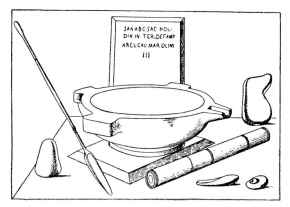

Tools used for encaustic, from the Roman painter's grave at St Médard-des-Prés

'Next . . . they fastened boards, shaped as triglyphs are now made, on the ends of the beams where they had been cut off in front, and painted them with blue wax.'[41]

What is undoubtedly meant here is cold wax paint, ready for painting, contrary to the following passage:

'But anybody who is more particular and who wants a polished finish of vermilion that will keep its proper colour, should, after the wall has been polished and is dry, apply with a brush punic wax, melted over a fire and mixed with a little oil: then after this he should bring the wax to a sweat by warming it and the wall at close quarters with charcoal enclosed in an iron vessel; and finally he should smooth it all off by rubbing it down with a wax candle and clean linen cloths, just as naked marble statues are treated. This process is called *Ganosis* in Greek. The protecting coat of punic wax prevents the light of the moon and the rays of the sun from licking up and drawing the colour out of such polished finishing.'[42]

Tools used for encaustic, from a mural painting at Pompeii (after Donner)

Wax was therefore only a protective covering, not a binding vehicle for the actual paint. Seen in this light the passage in Vitruvius on *Ganosis* does not contradict the well-known statement by Pliny that wax is not used for painting walls.

The Faiyum portraits are only a faint reflection of the splendour of the art of encaustic, now lost for ever, which flourished in Greece from the fourth century B.C. The only facts that have come down to us are the names of its supposed inventor, Aristides, and the greatest masters of the technique, outstanding among them Pausias, as well as highly laudatory descriptions of their masterpieces.

Encaustic played a leading role in Hellenistic and Roman panel painting, but it disappeared with the collapse of the ancient civilization. Only at the end of the nineteenth century was the interest in it revived. A number of wall paintings in the Berliner Stadtschloss dating from about 1800 are said to be painted with punic wax, and Boecklin painted a picture of Sappho in wax colours.

Hans Schmid, who is particularly concerned with the revival of encaustic today, prepares his encaustic colours in the form of pencils, bound with wax of his own preparation, and has invented tools which can be heated electrically. Kurt Wehlte, the well-known painter and expert on technique, and author of *Wandmalerei, Praktische Einführung in Werkstoffe und Techniken*, is especially interested in the purification of wax. Dr **A.** Stois of Munich has done very comprehensive work on beeswax and punic wax, and has supplied an exact recipe.[43]

Modern reconstructions of ancient techniques must necessarily be relative. Modern materials are often different from those used by the ancients; there are frequently gaps and ambiguities in the written sources. Finally, we are different people, with other opinions, ideas and ways of thinking.

Since it was not possible to work on the site intended for the paintings, it was decided to use panels to be inserted in the walls afterwards, similar to those at Pompeii.

The first two paintings in the cycle were executed on wood supports. We come now to the first one painted on plaster.

The fundamentally different grounds affected the method of the insertion; whereas the wooden panels had to be inserted with great care to prevent the natural moisture of the wall spreading to the wood, the transferring of the plaster panels was much less of a problem.

For the latter, iron frames about $1\frac{1}{4}$ inches deep were used to receive the plaster. These frames had thole-pins at the sides to give them the necessary grip on the wall. The iron parts were protected against rust with red oxide of lead and alumium paint, and the brick grid covered with a layer of fine plaster. This was keyed to give the next layer a firm support.

This ground formed the substitute for the wall in all the paintings of the cycle. The different rate of water accumulation affected the normal relationship between the rough rendering on the wall and the top layers.

The ground was a thick coat of plaster of Paris and fat lime, as used for partition walls. It was found to be impossible to divide these layers into a coarse rendering and a smoother top coat, because the top layer was lifted off by the brush with the hot wax. The most

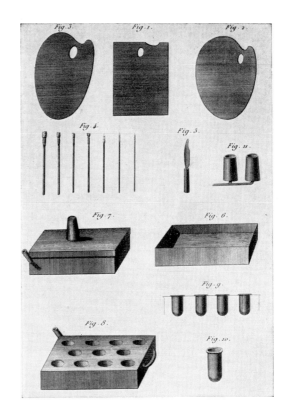

Tools used for encaustic, from Diderot d'Alembert,
'Encyclopédie'; end of the eighteenth century

reliable ground was found to be a diluted cement mortar neutralized with dilute sulphuric acid. The contours were indicated with unbound water paint and the surface was rubbed with cold wax, which was then inusted with a special hand tool.

It is worth noting that encaustic colours hardly change in drying. There is perhaps a suggestion of Pointillism, the technique which developed from Impressionism, where the dots of colour only give the desired impression when seen from a distance. The wax paint

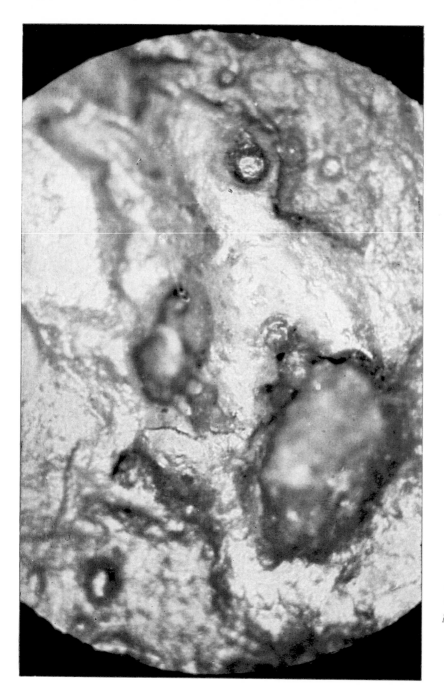

Mummy portrait, from el Faiyum.
Microphotograph of a detail of
picture opposite

Mummy portrait, from el Faiyum, Egypt. Encaustic. Original in the study collection of the author

Mummy portrait, from el Faiyum.
Microphotograph of a detail of
picture opposite

Mummy portrait, from el Faiyum. Tempera. Original in the study collection of the author. See the two preceding illustrations

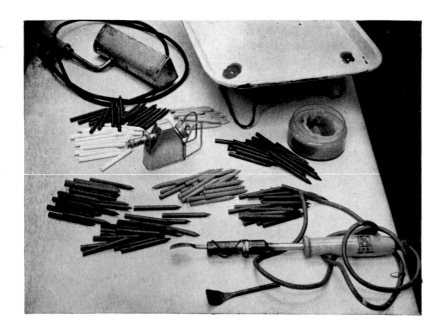

Tools and colours for painting with hot wax as used by Dr Hans Schmid

can be well glazed if it is moderately thinned with turpentine or spirit of turpentine. It can be applied in a thick consistency with a heated spatula (the cauterium of the Ancients), the broad side of the spoon being used for smoothing and the pointed end for incising or removing the paint. The slightly modelled surface of the Faiyum portraits was obtained with this technique.

The painting was now exposed to heat and inusted a second time, and in melting the contours became softened. For this we found the hand inusting tool preferable to a blow-torch. The surface now had a soft lustre, which was heightened by rubbing it with a

Above: Inustion of the cold waxed ground by means of an electric inusting tool. On the right, detail of sketch
Below: Surface of picture after application of wax colours.
Right: Sketch

Surface structure of the finished painting, enlarged

cloth. The unusual appearance of encaustic is caused by the light penetrating the slightly transparent wax.

The durability of encaustic interiors has been proved by surviving examples which date back 2000 to 4000 years, but it is not yet possible to say how well it will last out of doors, as the first experiments were only made a matter of decades ago.

POMPEIAN FRESCOES (STUCCO LUSTRO)

A complete reconstruction of ancient techniques is for many reasons impossible. This is especially so in the case of Pompeian wall paintings because the murals discovered at Pompeii were painted in various techniques and at various times. The earliest can be dated about 300 years earlier than the latest, which form the majority. It is natural that the technique should have changed during such a long period, as well as the style, and that individual artists and their workshops should have their own traditions and techniques.

Thus we must also restrict ourselves to one particular technique, the one we believe to be most characteristic of Pompeian wall painting. We have chosen the polished, ironed fresco and the reconstruction of this technique is probably the most important in our cycle.

The style chosen for the fresco was not taken from Pompeian wall painting, but from Greek vase decoration. The beautifully smooth fresco surface achieved in the reconstruction was reminiscent of a Greek vessel in our study collection. Although this was made three to four hundred years before Pompeii was built and is in a different technique, there appeared to be an affinity between the ironed fresco and the vase painting. Even the Greek clay plaque at Berlin, of which we own a copy, is an unusual size for clay. In a wider sense this plaque already comes under the category of wall painting, and although no examples of Greek mural painting survive, it is certain that it was very closely connected with vase painting.

With this question in mind we came across the following words of Professor Amedeo Maiuri:[44] 'Thanks to some small monochromes on marble at Herculaneum which bear the signatures of Greek artists of the first century B.C., we have been given a faint but pure and rare reflection of the technique and the paintings of the golden Hellenistic Age. One of these is the small and exquisite picture of women playing at knuckle bones, signed by Alexandros

Aristotle before the bust of Plato. Four sketches in outline and monochrome

the Athenian.' This painting shows the connection between Pompeii and Greek wall and vase painting.

Like the archaic works of the Homeric Age, this is greater art than the Roman copies of what are mostly late Hellenistic works. And as we were reluctant to iron a painting which set out to create an illusion of space and volume, a flat design in the spirit of Greek vase painting was chosen.

In the report which follows, not only the composition of each layer and the mixing, application and smoothing processes should be noted, but the importance of applying each layer at the right moment.

268

Method of Procedure

The brick grid was covered with a coat of rendering containing coarse river sand (this mixture corresponds to a high-class mortar for external work).

The first coat of sand mortar

Was composed of 3 parts coarse river sand and 1 part fat lime. The fat lime was measured in a thick consistency as it was cut from the pit, then sieved into the well-dried sand and thoroughly mixed with it. The application was five-sixteenths of an inch thick.

The second coat of sand mortar

Consisted of the same materials, and in the same quantities as the first coat except that the sand was finer, though a little coarser sand was also added. A coat five-sixteenths of an inch thick was applied to the first coat after an interval of twenty-four hours. It was smoothed with small wooden floats.

Stucco: The first coat

Was composed of 3 parts marble-dust and 1 part fat lime of thick consistency. After measuring, the latter was mixed with water, put through a fine sieve and well mixed with the marble-dust. A few pinches of sand were added. A layer one-eighth of an inch thick was applied to the mortar which was still damp, but firm.

The second coat

Just under one-eighth of an inch thick, was applied to the first coat after a delay of twelve to twenty-four hours. A wooden float was used for rubbing it smooth, but this could not be done until the stucco had taken on a matt appearance, i.e. had set, and the water had drained off the lower layers of the mortar.

Wetting the dry terra nova ground before application of plaster

*Upper and lower plaster coat,
keyed terra nova ground and brick
webbing in reverse order of
application*

A third coat, stained

Five-sixteenths of an inch thick, was applied with a decorator's brush. It consisted of 3 parts marble-dust, very finely sieved, and 1 part fat lime, also very finely sieved, and was stained with a light colour to be used as the ground.

Application of the final coat, or painting surface

Levelling the painting surface with a long wood float

The colours

Earth and mineral colours were used. They were stirred up in a thick consistency with medium and the mixture gradually thinned down for painting. The ground was applied with a large, soft brush. The tendency to stripiness can be avoided by stippling the paint on with a sponge which has been well squeezed out and then dipped in colour again. This paint was mixed with soap and potash, and was very easy to use. Naturally, we refrained from making any corrections whatever.

Ironing the surface of the painting

Once the colours had been mixed with soap, they could be ironed without the inter-mediate layer of paper recommended. The surface was first ironed, without using any pressure, immediately after the colours had been painted on the damp plaster; although painted on a wet ground, they did not peel off.

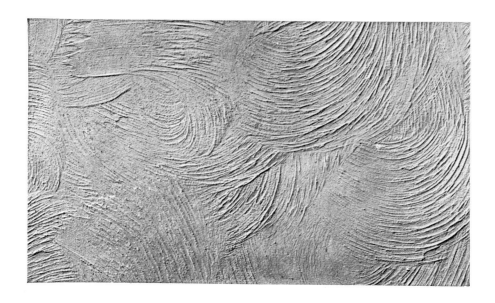

Surface of final coat of plaster, well set: later it is rubbed again with a piece of rough felt

Above: When the water has drained away from the lower layers, the surface is tested with a finger for set

Below: Application of third layer of fine plaster, which is tinted with colour. It is smoothed down cold with a steel trowel and overpainted with the colour of the ground

Medium (to be used with next application of paint)

60 gm. Marseilles soap (if not available, any high-grade soap) is scraped down, added to three-quarters of a pint distilled or rain-water and boiled until completely dissolved. 5 gm. potash is now added and the mixture heated again for short time. One pint lime-water is then added. Distilled water must be used on account of its softness and purity. The slight alkaline content of the soap makes the colours smooth and easy to iron. The effect of the potash is to prevent the soap from becoming flaky when the lime-water is added.

Intermediate stage showing contours drawn in and partly painted

Smoothing the finished painting with a hot iron

*The successive layers of
the painting exposed.
(Study for the final work)*

Detail of surface of finished painting, enlarged. Note the lines caused by particles of marble-dust being dragged along by the iron

Surface of a fragment of a mural painting from Pompeii. Note the same tracks made by ironing, running from top right to bottom left. Original in the study collection of the author

Testing the temperature of the iron

For testing, the iron is held close to the cheek. When the heat is just bearable the temperature is right. After twelve hours the surface was ironed again to drive the colours right into the surface.

Waxing: with the method formerly used to reconstruct the mirror-like lustre of the Ancients, the surface was treated again after six weeks, using wax dissolved in turpentine and heated in a double boiler.

To pass the hand over a stucco lustro surface is a delightful experience. This wonderfully smooth surface is unusually animated, suggestive of grandeur and costliness.

Among the studies we have dedicated to the Tektorium, those based on the recent experiments of Professor Kurt Wehlte[45] should also be mentioned. With the results of his examinations of the individual layers of antique frescoes, Wehlte has destroyed all previous assumptions regarding their composition and admixture, and the order in which they were applied. His studies aim to do away with the softness to be observed in the composition of more recent fresco layers. While it had been generally assumed hitherto that a proportion of 1 part lime to 3 parts sand was necessary for all the layers of mortar, Wehlte discovered that the proportions used were in fact different, namely, 1 part lime to $1\frac{1}{2}$ parts sand for the rendering, and 1 part lime to 1 part sand for the top layer. He also found that the coarseness of grain was different, and notably that the upper layers, not the lower, contained the coarser sand. In some of our test mortars on brick webbing in iron frames we followed the sand-grain sizes recommended by Wehlte. (Later we examined the hardness of the individual layers by exposing them again.)

Our experiments have been carried out in accordance with Wehlte's results,[45] and the various sands sorted by sieving, as shown in the illustration on page 284.

The finished fresco

Extracts from experiments in stucco lustro:

First layer: terra nova (not visible)

Second layer: 1½ parts lime
*   3 parts medium grain sand*

Third layer: Same composition as
*   second layer*

Fourth layer: 1 part lime
*   2½ parts fine grain sand*

Fifth layer: 1 part lime
*   2 parts marble-dust, with small*
*   quantity of sand added*

Sixth layer: Same composition as
*   fifth layer, but tinted grey*

Seventh layer: Coat of grey paint

Test strips of ten colours
commonly used in fresco
painting

Specimen of stucco lustro without wax treatment showing that colours can be ironed

Extracts from experiments in stucco lustro:

Same composition as corresponding layer in first specimen

Same composition as corresponding layer in first specimen

Same composition as corresponding layer in first specimen

Same composition as corresponding layer in first specimen

Ironed fresco. The figure on the central panel is added in secco

Specimen of stucco lustro without wax treatment, combined with secco.

Proportions of sand, brick-dust, and brick chips, after the experiments of Dr Wehlte (with slight variations)

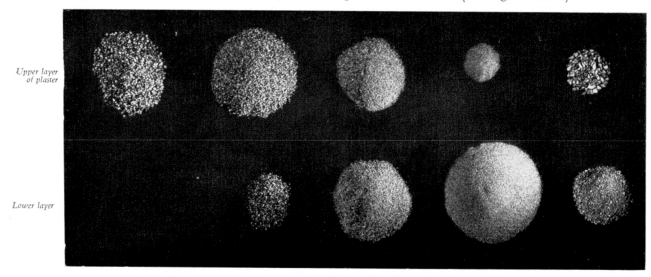

Upper layer
of plaster

Lower layer

Upper layer: Thickness 0·4—2·5 cm.★ : 1·5 parts sand to 1 part lime

	Sand 'd'	Sand 'a'	Sand 'b'	Sand 'c'	Brick Chips
	30·2%	46·5%	19·3%	3·7%	3·7%
Diameter:	more than 2 mm.	more than 1·2 mm.	more than 0·5 mm.	more than 0·2 mm.	up to 1 cm.

Undercoat: Thickness 0·4–2·5 cm. (*c.* 8 mm. for experiments): 1 part sand to 1 part lime

	Sand 'a'	Sand 'b'	Sand 'c'	Brick-dust★★
	7·4%	32·7%	51·5%	6·5%
Diameter:	more than 1·3mm.	more than 0·5 mm.	more than 0·2 mm.	medium fine

The remainder of 1·9% dust-fine sand was not taken into account, on the assumption that it would adhere to the coarser sand.

★Taken by the author as 8 mm.   ★★Used by author instead of sand.

Terra nova

Rough undercoat

Intermediate layer

Final surface

Painted surface

Specimen of fresco, showing layers, according to Professor Wehlte

Keyed terra nova layer; when set, this is soaked with thin lime-water, and then covered with the undercoat, which contains brick-dust

Intermediate layer, applied to undercoat when set

Finishing coat containing extra brick chips

This forms the ground for the fresco.

Undercoat

Intermediate coat

Upper layer

Final coat, containing marble-dust

Painted surface

Specimen of fresco, showing layers according to Professor Wehlte

Same as preceding specimen, except for addition of another final coat, composed as follows:

      1 part fine marble-dust
      $\frac{1}{4}$ part sand, grain size 'b'
      1 part lime

This layer is smoothed with a trowel, and provides the ground for the fresco.

Further specimens of exercises in stucco lustro, using Professor Wehlte's formula.

Undercoat

Intermediate layer

Layer containing potsherds

Layer containing marble-dust

Painted surface

Specimen of stucco lustro

Undercoat and intermediate layer.

Upper coat, without brick chips, containing potsherds up to *c.* 3 sq. cm. pressed into fresh plaster (to drain off water).

Final coat, containing marble-dust.

Fresco painting, soap added.

Smoothing with hot iron when colours set.

Experience proved that the potsherds, which, like the brick chips, had been soaked in water for 24 hours, kept the final coat so wet that painting could only be begun after a delay of 24 hours, and ironing only after a delay of 2 days.

Undercoat

Intermediate layer
of plaster

Upper layer of
plaster

First coat contain-
ing marble-dust

Second coat
containing marble-
dust, tinted

Specimen of stucco lustro

Undercoat and intermediate layer of plaster.
Upper layer of plaster.
First layer containing marble-dust.
Second layer containing marble-dust, tinted grey.
Fresco painting, with use of bland soap.
Ironing.

Specimen of stucco lustro

Undercoat: 1 part sand to 1 part lime.
Intermediate layer: lime plus $\frac{1}{4}$ part sand.
Upper coat, rough-grained from removal of
succeeding layers.
Smooth-cast of same composition as undercoat.
First layer containing marble: 1 part marble-dust,
$\frac{1}{4}$ part sand 'b'.
Thickness 3–4 mm.

Second layer containing marble-dust, tinted:
    1 part marble-dust,
    1 part lime,
    colour.
Thickness: 2 mm.
Third layer, containing marble-dust, tinted:
    Same composition as second layer.
Thickness: 1 mm.

Background and details painted in, using soap. When dry, surface is ironed with a very hot iron but using little pressure.

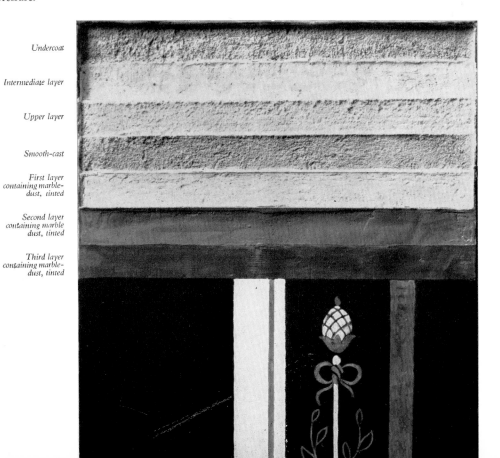

Undercoat

Intermediate layer

Upper layer

Smooth-cast

First layer
containing marble-
dust, tinted

Second layer
containing marble
dust, tinted

Third layer
containing marble-
dust, tinted

Specimen of oiled fresco

Undercoat	The same, oiled
Intermediate layer	Painting of background and details
Upper layer	Surface ironed with a hot iron
Layer containing marble-dust	

Undercoat

Intermediate layer

Upper layer

Top layer, containing marble-dust

The same, oiled

The Painter's Guide of Mount Athos, discovered by Didron, gives us a clear idea of Byzantine painting. This treatise lays down the strictest and most exact rules, enforced by dogma, on how the holy scenes should be represented.

It also prescribes the technical processes to be followed in fresco painting. What concerns us here is the description of the two layers of plaster, the lower one consisting of lime mixed with straw, and the upper one, lime mixed with tow (*opsis*). The passage runs as follows:

'§ 56. How to mix lime with straw: Take pure lime and throw it into a large container. Select some fine straw of medium strength, without dust. Stir it into the lime with a pick-handle. If it is too solid, add water to it until it has a workable consistency, then leave the mixture for two or three days, when it will be ready for application.

'§ 57. How to mix lime with tow. (*Opsis*.) Take the best slaked lime and put it into a small container. Take beaten tow, well cleaned of all bark. Turn it and fold it as if to make a thick rope out of it and then cut it up as fine as possible on a block with a hatchet; shake it well to get rid of the dust. [Then put the tow in a sieve], shake it lightly into the container, and stir it with a shovel or pick-handle. Do the same again as the first time, five or six times, until the lime [is so dry that it] does not crack any more. Leave it to ferment like the others, and you have *opsis*.'[46]

Eibner believes that the fibres were necessary because of the shallow layers required for vaults and apses. They kept the plaster damp for a long time and guaranteed that it remained firm and did not crack. The right proportion of fibres to plaster for both layers became evident in the course of the experiments.

In Egypt and the Far East, straw was also used in plaster, indeed sometimes in such large quantities as to be visible under the painting.

In reconstructing this technique two layers of equal thickness were used. The straw was freed of dust and cut into lengths of one-eighth to three-sixteenths inch with a hatchet and scissors.

The first coat was applied and levelled with a wood float. In the second layer, to prevent lumps from forming, the tow was mixed into the lime as loosely and evenly as possible. This was applied to the first layer after some hours; it was evened down with a thin wooden board and smoothed with a steel trowel.

The top layer remained so damp that it could not be painted on for four days (according to Didron it should be three days). The sinter which now formed had first to be removed with a brush and razor blade. All the same, the painting did not smear and even resisted vigorous rubbing. The colours dried correspondingly slowly with the plaster and lightened much less in the process than is to be expected on a very wet ground.

The rough sketch

Chopped straw and thick lime

The first coat, containing straw, is applied with a wood float

Levelling the first coat with a steel float

Cutting up the tow

Separating the tow

Above: Applying the second layer or 'opsis', containing tow

Below: Levelling the second layer, with upward movement

The two main problems to be solved in prehistoric painting are firstly, the technique in which the paintings were executed, and secondly, the conditions to which they owe their preservation to the present day.

We have already attempted several ways of solving these questions with reference to the Spanish rock paintings.[47] The hitherto scattered evidence was collected and weighed and an attempt made to identify the technique used by laying hold of isolated details of the painting methods. To facilitate this, use was also made of specimens of works by primitive peoples whose level of culture is still that of the Stone Age. Finally, an attempt was made to reconstruct the techniques in practice.

These practical experiments, described here in detail, are of particular significance. Not only did they provide an opportunity to test all sorts of hypotheses on ground, media, and methods of application, but they also permitted us to study comprehensively the expressive qualities of the techniques thus discovered. Detailed accounts are given of the various experiments with fat, blood, and vegetable media, and the conclusion reached was, that the part played by the binding medium for the painting process as well as for the preservation of the paintings, is much smaller than hitherto assumed. It appears that in the case of the Spanish paintings, the painting method, as well as the extraordinarily good state of preservation, was determined rather by geological and climatic conditions, especially by the dampness of the stone. In the reconstruction experiments it was found that the colour

Dish of volcanic trachyte from Anval

also adhered to damp stone without a medium. Indeed, the media could not have been decisively important for preservation for the simple reason that they themselves have not survived the long stretch of time which elapsed until the paintings were rediscovered, so that no proof by analysis is now possible. Their preservation seems to be due rather to a process of sintering, i.e. the formation of a 'natural fresco', and to the evenness of temperature in the caves due to the fact that they were sealed off.

The most important of the Spanish rock paintings have been reproduced here, mostly in colour, and a survey given of their stylistic development.

THE FRANCO-CANTABRIAN PAINTINGS

The grease painting theory

The modern theories on the technique of the Franco-Cantabrian paintings are based on the work of Henri Breuil and Hugo Obermaier.[48]

'The pigments used by the artists were vegetable charcoal, which was found locally in large quantities, as well as ochre and hematite: these give all shades of red, yellow, and brown.

298

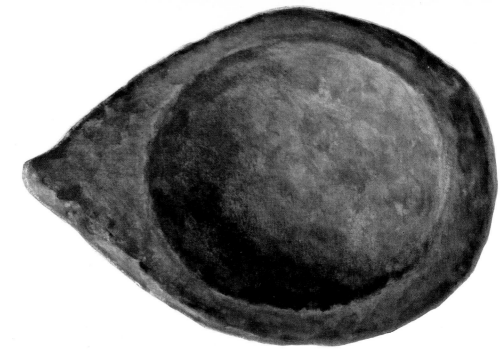

Two views of a lamp (?), from the Dordogne
(From 'Dokumente zur Malstoffgeschichte', by Kurt Herberts)

Often the pieces of colour are sharpened like pencils. There is no blue or green, but there are shades of violet, probably produced with some kind of manganiferous mineral. The pigment was usually ground to a fine powder and either animal fat or vegetable juices added to it so that a viscous paste was formed which could be applied with the finger or with a proper brush. The brushes consisted of hair, feathers or little pieces of wood, dipped in fat. As the paint was applied direct to the surface of the rock this could be done only when the rock was dry and by using viscous substances like fat or resin, and these materials could only be used if they were heated. In this way real oil paintings were created which combined with the surface of the rock and are excellently preserved. The incisions were made with flint tools, scrapers, or sharpened flints, and in the same way the drawings were worked in clay, or they were incised with the finger or a piece of wood.'

According to Breuil and Obermaier, therefore, the paintings were executed with grease or resin paint. In fact they are frankly called oil paintings. But this claim has no chemical foundation. Neither fat nor resin remnants have been found, and it must therefore be made clear that their assumptions do not rest on facts, as this passage would seem to imply, but only on conjectures. They are based on the following evidence:

1. The stone dishes found, described by Breuil and Obermaier as a kind of mortar, which are supposed still to contain sediments of greasy colour paste, and
2. More particularly, the impression produced by the paintings themselves.
3. I should like to add another reason which, though not admitted, was understandably at the back of their minds, namely, that they have subconsciously judged the technique from the point of view of the state of preservation of the works—and it is commonly supposed that oil paint is the most durable.

But there is no proof that these little vessels were in fact meant for mixing colours. Other scholars have described them as lamps, on account of the similarity of shape with antique

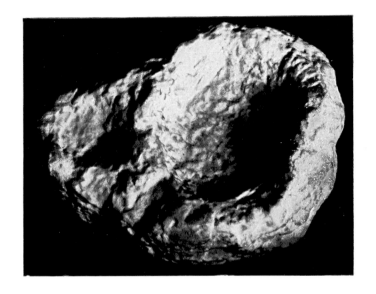

Palaeolithic lamp, from the Dordogne (copy). **In the study** *collection of the author*

clay lamps. Since the caves were dark, artificial light was essential, and there is no reason why these people should not already have had lamps. Boudon, who has made a special study of prehistoric lamps, mentions more than ten of these found in caves. It is very improbable that these lamps could have still contained remnants of grease, for an organic medium like fat could hardly be analysable, or even recognizable, after such a long time. Apart from this, fat and oleous media would have quickly saponified in the conditions which prevailed in the caves. The theory that organic media are now no longer verifiable is also confirmed by Dr A. Stois of Munich, who has assured us that an analysis for this purpose of fragments from eastern Spanish paintings yielded no relevant data from an analytical standpoint. Where organic substances were present the reactions were positive even in places where there was no paint and were due to other organic substances.

Even so, the grease-painting theory should not be dismissed out of hand, and one of the reasons for considering it is the clue provided by the practice of painting the body. It is an open question whether the little bowls which have been found—be they lamps or mixing-bowls for paint—may not eventually be considered to be pans for cosmetics; in any case it may be assumed[49] that the painting of the body is the first and original form of painting. The burial of bodies on pulverized red earth also throws light on the use of colour in connection with the human body. The bodies were sprinkled with pulverized colour for ritual purposes and not strictly for ornamentation. Thus it is proved that the earliest use of colour was for the burial of corpses. All the skeletons which have been found were embedded in red ochre. The red colour covers the bones, all the grave accessories and the surrounding stones. It even adheres to the shells which the dead man wore round his neck as an ornament. Consequently this is the first time that we see colour used purely in powder form, i.e. without the use of a medium. The tattooing still practised by primitive peoples should also be placed in this category; it consists of the injection of a pigment which shines through the skin and once the inflammation has healed is indelible. Similarly, we know that primitive peoples, like the tribes of the Upper Nile, paint their bodies by rubbing them with dry colours, for instance with ash.

Painting the body is a practice still to be found among primitive peoples today. Its purpose is to emphasize certain parts of the body and make them seem more important; it probably also serves as an insignia of a particular tribe, in so far, indeed, as it was not originally of magical significance. The body is either decorated with stripes and symbols, or patterned all over.

Whether cosmetics, that is, pigments bound with fat, can be assumed to have been used for this purpose in the Ice Age is still open to debate. Many primitive peoples bind the colours used for painting the body with fat; various tribes in South Africa, for instance, produce butter not as a food, but exclusively for body-paint.

Receptacle containing remains of red colour, from Anval (Canton de Chic le Comte)

It would seem permissible to conclude from this that the men of the Ice Age also used cosmetics, i.e. grease-bound pigments, to paint their bodies. But it is without doubt a far cry from this kind of painting to painting on walls. Perhaps there were intermediate stages of which no evidence remains, such as the painting of clothing, skins, basket-work, wooden tools (which certainly existed), and wooden weapons. In these cases paint would have been used as a method of protection and preservation. (Some kind of material must also have been used for attaching handles to stone axes; probably, besides being bound, these were cemented in with resinous substances.)[50] It is therefore probable that fat in the form of a cosmetic was used by Ice Age man for the painting of the body. Though it would be understandable to find it used for mural painting deriving from its use for body decoration, there are other reasons against this. In any case, no trace of this fat exists today, nor can it be proved by analysis to have existed.

The palimpsest technique and the question of grounds

On a number of these paintings a curious phenomenon was observed. Some of them are at first sight incomprehensible if assumed to be but a single layer. The parts of the animals are confused and do not form a whole, so that they seem to be completely disconnected. But if the line of one head, leg, or backbone is followed through it soon becomes evident that these are not disconnected pieces, but complete representations, only that they are in several layers. (The term for this phenomenon is 'palimpsest'.) What is the explanation of this? One would like to assume that either the artist was short of space, which is unlikely, or that it was a matter of reconsecrating the same spot with a new animal painting. The fact that these superimposed pictures of animals are not very clearly distinguishable from each other leads to the following deduction. At first sight it seems unlikely that the new animal painting should have been executed directly on top of an old one, and it is fairly safe to assume that the first representation was covered over, even if only with a light layer of pigment containing no medium, i.e. with powder colour. This would also seem to be more practical because it would be irritating to have to paint straight on top of the old picture. Now it is quite possible that the lower picture should work its way through in the course of time, and similar examples can be mentioned in the case of paintings by primitive peoples. To quote the report of the Frobenius expedition on bark and rock paintings in north-western Australia:

'The method for making bark and rock paintings never varies. First a white ground is applied. For this the painter takes some pipe-clay in his mouth, then fills his mouth with water and moves his tongue around until the clay is dissolved; then he blows hard so that

*Example of one area
painted several times over
(Palimpsest): Altamira*

the solution is sprayed over the surface of the bark or rock. The paint dries immediately in the extreme heat. In the rock paintings the outlines of the old picture are still clearly recognizable under the white coating.'

Since theories on intermediate layers in Ice Age paintings must necessarily remain hypothetical, this point has been mentioned only for the sake of completeness, not to draw any further conclusions from it.

The pastel technique and pigments

While there is little that we can say with certainty about liquid or impasto paint, we have some concrete evidence for the pictures painted in what, in fact, is a kind of pastel technique. In the grottoes of Eyzies and Font-de-Gaume, red ochre has been found in the form of triangular or egg-shaped fragments. These fragments have been given a definite shape. The triangular ones are particularly frequent; they are carefully formed and some of them have a hole so that they can be hung up, or hung round the neck. Most of them are of red ochre. There are also pieces of ochre sharpened to a point; some are more or less blunt, others are long, like proper pencils. The pieces which are of a soft material and have been sharpened, look as if they had been used for drawing. A real pencil with a slightly used point, found at Font-de-Gaume, is of particular interest.

The ochrous material was found in the vicinity of the caves. Numerous hoards of ochrous clay, yellow or red, and sometimes black, as well as fragments of iron and manganese ores of the same colours, have been discovered there. It was a simple matter for prehistoric man to collect suitable pieces from runnels formed in the ground by rain.[51] Examples from historical times show that pastels applied to walls without the use of a medium may last a very long time. One need only think of the monumental pastels mentioned and recommended by Ostwald, and described by Eibner in his book on mural painting, to realize that even this age of highly advanced techniques can learn this from most primitive times.

Here we touch on the question of pigments and for the sake of completeness these are listed below. All are natural colours in earth or stone form. Red ochre was mostly used for the simple pictures. It is also the most prominent in the later works and appears in various tones ranging from pale yellow to dark brown (see pp. 310–311). Apart from ochre there is themaite, which often appears in the form of a micaceous ore in mica slate and gneiss, a hexagonal-rhomboid mineral. Its colour ranges from iron-black to dark steel-grey. The thin laminae of iron mica are reddish-yellow to dark red, particularly in the strata of crystalline slate. Vegetable charcoal was also used. All colours, from pale yellow to black, via red and brown, were obtained from these minerals. Blue and green do not occur; their use was not known. It is extraordinary to find violet occurring, and Obermaier's recent assumption that this colour was brought about by the changing of another colour with the course of time, seems a reasonable one.

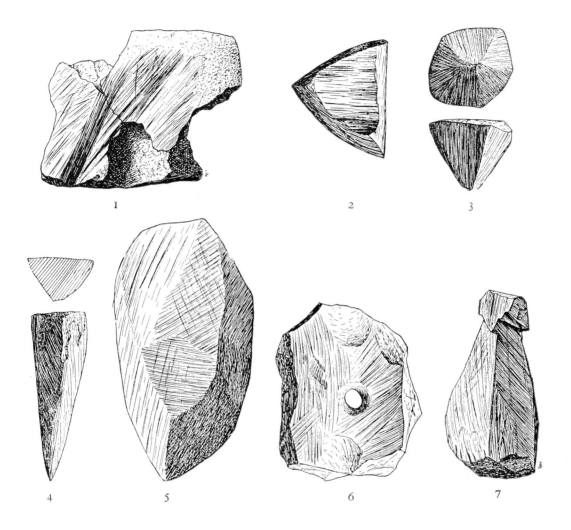

1. Fragment of worked manganese (*Cave of Eyzies*)

2 and 3. Piece of worked red ochre (*Eyzies*)

4. Pieces of red ochre shaped into form of a pencil (*Laugerie Haute*)

5. Piece of worked red ochre (*Cave of Placard*)

6 and 7. Pieces of red ochre, one with hole, the other with one thick end, (?) to be used as pendants (*Eyzies and St Martory*)

Practical attempts to reconstruct the assumed techniques of prehistoric cave paintings

Our investigations of the theories on possible techniques and painting methods used in prehistoric rock paintings leave many questions unanswered. In order to find a criterion of judgment and prove one theory correct, it was decided in addition to attempt to reconstruct these techniques in practice. In order to serve this purpose, such reconstructions would have to be carried out as far as possible under the same conditions as the originals. There was therefore no question of a copy which merely imitated their outer appearance, but executed in modern techniques such as oil paint on canvas or watercolour on paper; the original conditions had to be observed as far as they could be judged. These were as follows:

1. With the help of a geologist a piece of stone obtained from the cave of Altamira was tested for the nearest kind of stone to be found in Germany. A travertine (calcium carbonate), found near Bad Canstatt, was finally chosen.

2. All the pigments had to be found in a natural state and in the same colours, ranging from yellow via red to nearly black, as they were used in the originals, and if possible, in the same form as found in Franco-Cantabria or eastern Spain.

3. Since the reconstructions could not be carried out in Spain, the copies made *in situ* by the Kulturmorphologisches Institut in Frankfurt (the Frobenius Institute) were taken as a point of departure. Our thanks are due to the Frobenius Institute for their kind co-operation.

1. *Style*

    Reconstruction of

    (*a*) Outline pictures of the Aurignacian period.

    (*b*) Stipple paintings of the same epoch.

    (*c*) The developed two-colour style of the Magdalenian period.

2. *Technique*

   (*a*) Lumps of dry colour, i.e. a pastel-like application.

   (*b*) Ground colours bound with a watery medium, either of thick or of thin consistency.

   (*c*) Clayey, paste-like medium.

   (*d*) Thin, flowing colours bound with blood or honey.

   (*e*) Colours bound with grease.

3. *Tools*

   (*a*) The human hand.

   (*b*) Twigs with frayed ends, tufts, birds' feathers, and bunches of fur, some with primitive handles.

To record our results and experiences in a straightforward report proved to be impossible. Since isolated details formed the point of departure for these reconstructions, and fresh problems constantly had to be considered, it seemed more to the point to record the results directly in the sections on the individual techniques.

To begin with, practice tests of the style and technique of the originals were made on cardboard, grounded with sand to give it something like the surface of the stone. In this way the technical and artistic spirit of the originals was recaptured, and the forms were now executed on the stone itself. The preliminary test-pieces ensured that the reconstruction would not be a copy made to a formula, but would combine accuracy with the lively execution of the original. Details of the results obtained are given below.

Problems relating to grounds

It soon became apparent that the moisture of the rock was of fundamental importance. This question cropped up again and again during the course of the reconstruction and

Manganese ore (product of efflorescence)
Brown hematite (brown iron ore)
Hematite (bloodstone, iron oxide)

Pyrolusite
Cyprian umber
Brown clay ironstone (umber)

Pyrolusite (manganese ore, brownstone)
Pea ore, or oolitic limonite (manganiferous)

All pieces in the study collection of the au

Soft iron ochre, medium tone
Red ochre (ruddle)
Red pea ore

Bauxite, medium tone
Bog iron ore
Bauxite, light tone

Iron ochre, fairly dark
Iron ochre, very light
Iron ochre, dark

every time it was the practical approach which brought it to the fore. Up to then the need of a dry ground had been taken for granted.[52] The fact that the paintings discovered in the drier caves were in a worse state of preservation, or destroyed altogether, is quite independent of this. From this, conclusions may also be drawn about the technique by which they are painted, and consequently their state of preservation.

Practical experiments show that we cannot assume the existence of a painting ground laid on the damp stone, as the subsequent layers would not have produced a primary effect. This agrees with the view that the Franco-Cantabrian paintings were painted *al prima* on to the rock, and the fact that the colour sank in well and integrated closely with the rock, is proof that this could be done with very good results.

The pastel technique

For our experiments we used the natural lumps of colour described above. If it can be taken as proved that the colour had been rasped and scraped off these lumps, and then, presumably, ground completely to powder, then it may be assumed without further ado that this powder had been used either to rub into the body, made into a cosmetic for the same purpose, or made into liquid paint. Still, the sharpened lumps, though in the minority, were obviously used to draw with directly like pastels, although to draw on dry stone with such lumps proved unsatisfactory, since the colour only adhered lightly to the bumps in the surface of the rock, and to draw with them was very difficult. On damp stone this technique was more successful; but even then the colour did not penetrate into the pores of the stone, so that there was still a difference between the original pictures and the reconstructions. Now experiments were made to float and dissipate the particles of pigment by keeping the test-pieces damp in order to obtain a more thorough integration with the stone. Though this was only partially successful, it may be assumed that the colour ran in the course of time and was washed into the pores of the stone, as is in many cases still visible in the original paintings. There are examples of what presumably is such a process at and near Altamira, but the extent of it probably varied locally.

It should not, however, be overlooked that the effect of the water on the colour was not only to dissolve and dissipate it, but to create new layers of lime on top of the painted surface, either deposited from below, or by continuous or periodic sintering. This process prevented the colours from being washed off and at the same time helped to preserve the works. A detailed discussion of these processes follows later.

Until now the terms 'drawn', 'painted', or 'painted with flat wash'[48] have been used to describe the techniques in which these rock paintings were produced. But these terms are really of a more general nature; this is evident since they are used to describe the pictures in their present state, for these naturally bear the marks of time, and the way is thus left open for numerous interpretations on the technique. However, it is dangerous to draw too definite conclusions in retrospect. Thus we cannot simply say that a picture is drawn because it consists of outlines, that it has been painted in a flat technique just because it consists of broad contours, or that a flat wash has been used because we see larger areas of colour. Similarly, we must not assume hastily that the outline pictures executed in pastel technique are the most primitive just because they are the earliest at present known to us. Although such conclusions may possibly agree with the facts, they are not bound to do so. In any case the practical reconstruction showed not only the possibility of using the pastel technique, on dry or damp stone, but that equally good, or even better results are obtained with liquid colour, as described in detail below. This ought to provide a strong case for the mediumless technique.

To sum up, the reconstruction of the pastel technique, that is, a mediumless technique, appears to suggest that it was employed at least in part for the early, as well as for the later, richer styles.

The use of colour in paste form

The experiments revealed that it is difficult to apply the colour in the form of a paste. Colour paste bound only with water will not cohere, and so cannot be considered. Suet of deer or other fats were equally unsatisfactory. Application with the finger must be counted out because the paste is too thin. Even small pads of fur were so unsatisfactory that paint in this consistency can hardly be considered, if at all. There is one exception. The hinds of Covalanas painted in a stippling technique may just possibly have been executed in this kind of paint, since the method of application is interrupted, because of the necessity of refilling the tool. But there is no proof of this, and on the whole the use of paint in the form of a paste must be considered unlikely.

The use of fat as a binding medium

Fat has a fairly thick consistency, and would have had to be used as a binding medium for the colour paste, whose use, however, we consider unlikely. But if fat is heated it can be used in liquid form. Bowls containing the remains of colours have been found near hearths, and one expert has drawn the obvious conclusions from this. However, the necessity of constantly keeping the mixture of colour and fat warm, makes this unlikely. We need only remember that the positions in which the artist painted were often very awkward; he had to kneel, squat, and lie, as well as work by artificial light. If he was far away from the hearth it must have been almost impossible to keep the paint warm, though it might conceivably have been possible to keep a stone dish hot if the skilful use of the flame of a stone lamp or an ordinary small fire is considered. This procedure would resemble that used for the Greek encaustic technique.

But grease paint applied hot presented insuperable difficulties when it came to painting on damp stone. Since water repels fat it did not adhere well enough, the paint formed small balls on contact with the moisture and thus also lost its cohesion. In addition it saponified

314

Specimen showing the progressive darkening of blood.
Animal's blood is painted on the stone in the form
of a T.
The identical colour, in thick light-proof carmine
watercolour, is painted beside it.
Whereas the blood soon darkens and becomes
browner, the watercolour keeps its original colour.
With time, the blood will become still dirtier in
tone until it is almost black

on contact with calcareous water so that the process of cohesion was hindered even more.

The same applies to other animal fats like suet, bone marrow, and fish-oil, so that their use has not been considered here and no allowances made for them in the experiments. Likewise with the resin, which though possibly used for binding axes, could not have been used as a painting medium for lack of a solvent. Wax, which, like animal fat, would have had to be used hot, can also be excluded.

The use of blood as a binding medium

In view of the magic significance of the paintings, one must at least consider the possibility of the use of blood. Apart from its property of sticking and clotting, which may or may not have been known, the colour of blood may have had an attraction. Besides, blood is still used by primitive peoples and even by European peasants.[53] (*N.B.* Blood must be stirred immediately, or it clots and becomes useless.)

It turned out to be quite possible to mix blood with powdered pigment and apply it to stone, and to dilute it with water. As with nearly all methods of applying liquid paint, the application presented no problem. The mixture combined well with dry, as well as damp,

315

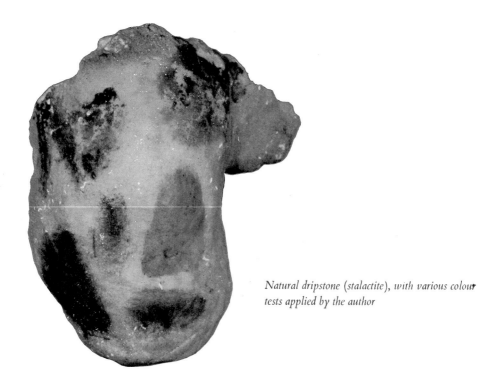

Natural dripstone (stalactite), with various colour tests applied by the author

stone. In the latter case the paint penetrated deeper into the pores of the stone, which seems to be a great advantage.

It should not be forgotten that blood does not remain red but soon blackens (see the illustration on p. 315), so that the lighter tones of yellow ochre eventually blackened too.

Vegetable binding media

The difficulties involved in obtaining and preparing vegetable binding media presuppose mental processes of which we can scarcely imagine primitive man to have been capable. The plants would have had to be either pressed, as, for instance, milk-weed (genus *Euphorbia*), whose juice has adhesive qualities, or else cooked. The juice of berries has no adhesive properties, and is too insubstantial for the stone, though it may have been used on wood or matting, as indeed it is by primitive peoples today. The mosses found in the tundra on the outlying ice-regions would have had to be cooked to be useful as a painting medium. Icelandic moss is still manufactured in Germany into a starch-containing gum, and is occasionally used as a medium for simple interior decoration. Although man of the Ice Age used fire, cooking was unknown to him because the necessary vessels did not exist. Thus, the possibility that vegetable media were used is small. A more likely substance is honey, because—as the picture of the honey-gatherer shows (though in connection with the eastern Spanish culture)—honey was known and can be used without difficult preparation. Besides, it has good binding properties and dissolves easily in water.

The use of liquid colour

Although it has been suggested here that the pastel technique, which requires no medium, doubtless had a certain use, liquid paint seems to be a more likely material. Liquid colours are easily applied with bunches of feathers or hairs, or, more primitively still, with the chewed end of a stick, as is the practice among the aborigines of Australia. The experiments showed that small pads of fur are also serviceable. Whereas the paint would run down a vertically held brush in painting ceilings, these pads of fur, because of their sponginess, would have been very suitable for this purpose and must be seriously considered. As a matter of fact, the tools used will never be identified for certain, because fur and feathers were probably also employed for head-dresses, clothes, and ornaments.

But if the results of our experiments lead us to conclude that liquid paint was the most likely material, we must not make the mistake of thinking that it was used in a very liquid form. The stone was always damp, so that the effectiveness of very liquid paint would have been small. (On the other hand, it was found that thoroughly damp stone, in contrast to dry, took up the paint in quite a different way, and in fact more satisfactorily.) Only on dry stone—and this must have been the exception—could very thin paint have been used, since the dry porous stone absorbs large quantities of liquid which it draws out of the pigment. With dry stone, therefore, there was the danger that the pigment might remain on the surface of the rock as a loose dry powder and exposed to the danger of flaking or being blown off. Here must be mentioned—last, but not least—the results obtained with water alone. This experiment confirmed what we have already said, namely, that good reconstructions with a technique using water were possible in all the styles of the originals; the mediumless technique therefore has to be considered.

The mixed technique

The pictures of animals from the ceiling of Altamira, painted in the highly developed two-colour technique, could not be accurately reconstructed with the stone available because the protuberances in the rock, which helped to give the animals actual plasticity in the originals, were lacking. Even if we had a rock with such an uneven surface an accurate copy would still have presented certain difficulties, for the parts affected by sintering, a process which took many millennia, could not have been reconstructed. We had to be content with a surface which would present the best compromise.

Our reconstruction established that these representations of animals could also have been executed in a mixed technique, part pastel and part liquid colour. It is known that the images were first engraved into the rock with stone implements to emphasize the shapes of the animals, provided by the naturally formed and coloured rock. Only then was the first paint applied. The practical copyist would find it logical to use red to draw in the main shapes, whilst other experts have suggested that black was used for this preliminary drawing. However, it seems more likely that black was used at the end in order to increase the expressiveness of the work. It is of course possible that in isolated cases it may have been used for the first drawing-in; but though the question of which colour was used first in this

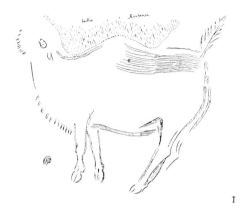

1

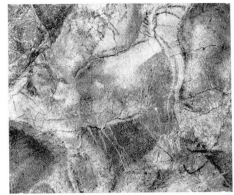

4

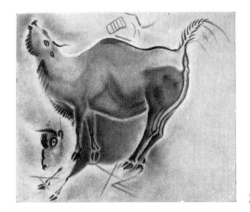

2

3

Four versions of a bison cow from the great ceiling of Altamira

1. *The preliminary engraved drawing, taken from the colour reproduction*
2. *Photograph of the original*
3. *Rendering in colour by H. Breuil*
4. *Reconstruction in original technique by the author*

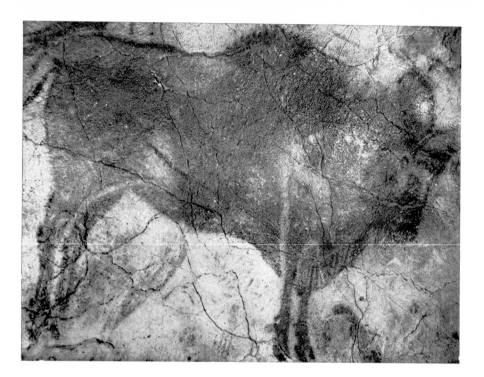

Four versions of a bison from Altamira

1. Photograph of the original

2. Copy from the original, by the Frobenius Institute, Frankfurt-am-Main

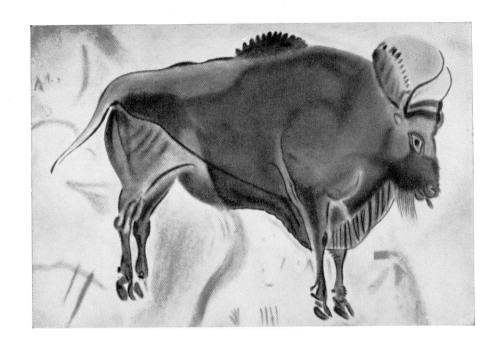

3. Rendering by H. Breuil

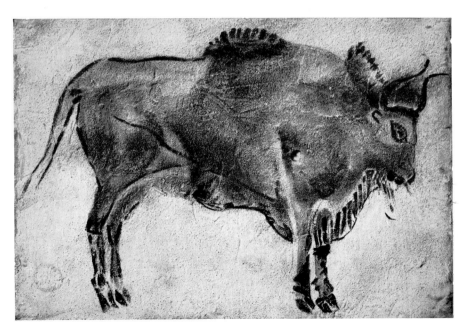

4. Reconstruction in original technique by the author

or that picture may have significance for judging the psychological approach of the artist, it does seem not to have any far-reaching consequences from a purely technical point of view.

Doubtless the pictures executed in the developed two-coloured style are of the highest expressive power and of a unique monumentality. But in their present state we are hardly justified in interpreting them in the way that Breuil has done in his copies. On the contrary, our reconstructions suggested that the originals were probably rather more elementary in expression. The painter was influenced to a great extent by the natural formation of the rock which, both then and now, is also essential to the appearance of the paintings. These views are borne out by the copies made from the originals by the Frobenius expedition and put at our disposal by the Kulturmorphologisches Institut in Frankfurt, for these copies also show a greater directness of expression and form (see illustrations on pp. 319–21).

The great skill of the Ice Age artist, even in the Magdalenian period, lies in the fact that each representation was a unique work. Thus, each different process was a finished statement in itself, though the artist's ability increased with constant practice. In this connection should be mentioned the small fragments of stone containing engraved drawings, which used to be regarded as preliminary studies for the larger works. Even if these were occasionally used as studies, however, they can hardly have been made for this purpose in the first instance. There is also the still unsolved problem of whether the ceiling of Altamira was painted by a few individuals or by perhaps whole generations or kin over a period of time, inspired again and again by hunting magic and by the magic force of their cults. Whether there were, as some experts, e.g. Kühn, believe, 'schools' which passed down their knowledge, is debatable. Certain circumstances speak in favour of such a view. On the other hand, it would not explain works of the size and magnificence of the Altamira ceiling, for these depend on a love of life and a vigour which could not have been passed on by tradition.

In conclusion, we were left with the impression that the pictures in the developed two-colour technique were executed in every kind of material available. The artists engraved, and probably worked extensively with liquid colour, as well as with dry lumps of colour, mixing them according to necessity, but unified them to create a magnificent harmony.

The puzzle of preservation and its circumstances

The experiments carried out so far have yielded a number of facts. We have been given an indication of the method of painting used. We have advanced to assumptions about the likely techniques. Through the experience gained by the attempts to reconstruct these techniques, our hypotheses have been given a basis of fact. The question of the preservation of the paintings has purposely been omitted until now in order to avoid the temptations of preconception.

In the next section the theories which may help us in solving this puzzling fact will be summarized. This will involve considering the whole environment in which they were created, as well as the geological and physical conditions which contributed to their preservation.

The Great Ice Age and the sequence of the Palaeolithic cultures

According to Gustav Riek there are seventeen theories about the Great Ice Age, to the last phase of which our paintings belong. Several experts have based their theories on the changes in the eccentricity of the earth's orbit, others on the obliquity of the elliptic and the wandering of the poles. Milankovitch has worked out a curve of solar radiation, which, as Riek says, has very considerably widened our knowledge of the evolution of the diluvium. The curve for the last 60,000 years shows four pairs of extreme cold waves, which fit in surprisingly well with the geologically founded division of the Ice Age into four glacial stages—Günz, Mindel, Riss, and Würm—based on glacial sedimentation, with the intermediate warmer interglacial periods,[54] and further climatic stages.

This nomenclature and subdivision of the Great Ice Age is completely valid for the lands lying on the northern approaches to the Alps, but it is also generally workable.

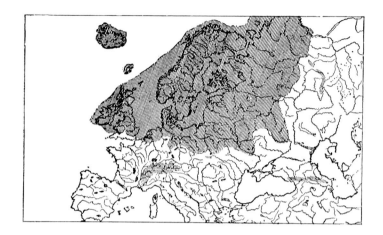

Map of Europe in the Ice Age at the time of maximum glaciation

Neanderthal man and the Lower Palaeolithic Age

The remains of the skeleton of Neanderthal and other species of primitive man and of his tools are divided into various periods as shown in the illustration. The age of Neanderthal man is called Lower Palaeolithic (earlier Palaeolithic Age), a period which can be determined from skull formation, such as the lack of chin, the low forehead, and the prominent eyebrow ridges which typify Neanderthal man. The various progressive stages of culture, called, after the French places where stone tools have been found, Prechellean, Chellean, Acheulean, Mousterian, can be determined according to the method of shaping the tools, whether they are only rough-hewn wedges or proper axes with handles, and whether blades, scrapers, scratching tools, etc., are already in use. These phases constitute the Lower Palaeolithic culture. They are also determined with the aid of animal remains found with the tools, which are classified according to the kind of climate they lived in and their stage of evolution and the strata in which they occur. These strata, or culture stages, vary in thickness and are sometimes only 4 in. deep.

324

Tools used by primitive species of man: ('homo heidelbergensis', 'homo steinheimensis', 'homo neandertalensis')

Prechellean   Chellean   Acheulean   Mousterian

Tools used by 'homo sapiens':

Aurignacian   Solutrean   Magdalenian   Late Stone Age   bone tool   Bronze Age
                                             axe with handle   axe

From the study collection of the author

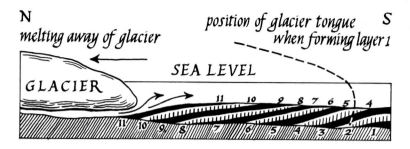

Formation of strata by sedimentation, after de Ger

'Homo Sapiens' and the Upper Palaeolithic culture

At the height of the last (Würm) glaciation period, during a fairly short interstadial (period of stationary ice) of slightly warmer climate, Neanderthal man was superseded by *homo sapiens*, the human of today. With this development the very first works of art appear.

The first period of *homo sapiens* is called the Upper Palaeolithic, or Late Palaeolithic Age. Tools are now no longer exclusively of stone, but also bone and horn, and are more highly developed. (No wooden tools have been preserved.) This period is subdivided as follows:

(*a*) Aurignacian (beginnings of painting: simple outline drawings, etc.).

(*b*) Solutrean.

(*c*) Magdalenian (greatest achievements in painting: Altamira ceiling, etc.).

(*d*) Azilian and Tardenoisian (last phase of Upper Palaeolithic Age).

These classifications apply mainly to the Franco-Cantabrian paintings. The corresponding culture for the Mediterranean area, which includes the paintings in eastern Spain, is known as the Capsian. Now follow the Mesolithic and Neolithic Ages, but these are outside the scope of this work because their artistic productions, in as far as they exist, are limited to symbolic signs, or, as in the case of eastern Spain, have become degenerate.

Dating the paintings

The oldest paintings date from the Würm glaciation period. This is proved by the finding of bones of animals living in a cold climate, such as mammoths, which are also depicted in the paintings. The later paintings, however, definitely belong to the period when the ice was finally retreating. This is the beginning of our present climate. The paintings with which we are concerned can now be dated with reasonable certainty to a period between 10,000 and 20,000 years ago. According to de Ger's system, based on the sedimentations of the post-Glacial Age, the earliest paintings of the Aurignacian period can be dated about 12,000 B.C. and the highly developed animal paintings of the Magdalenian about 8000 to 6000 B.C.

The origin of the caves

The caves and niche formations of the Franco-Cantabrian region were formed by rain-water seeping through cracks and crevices in the surface and dissolving the originally compact limestone to form soluble calcium bicarbonate (this process could not have taken place in case of sandstone, slate, or any primary rocks like granite or gneiss). Eventually hollows were formed which were then enlarged by corrosion, and their shape changed by the fragments which were continually falling from the ceiling and piling up on the floor of the cave. In the course of time clay was also washed in from outside and the sedimentations formed in this way are the strata in which the artefacts of the successive stages of culture were found embedded.

The exposed limestone ranges were sometimes composed of various different kinds of rock and weathered unevenly. Clayey deposits were destroyed more quickly than pure limestone so that eventually this jutted out over the softer clay. This is the origin of the overhangs below which were painted some of the eastern Spanish paintings, i.e. those not executed on completely exposed rock faces.

Why the prehistoric paintings have been preserved

The importance of moist air and a moist painting ground for the preservation of these paintings has been demonstrated by the work of Hugo Obermaier.[55] When excavating the cave of Altamira (1928–32) he checked the dampness of the rock and found that since their examination by Breuil in 1903 the paintings had suffered more from damp than ever before. The reason was found to be the existence above the paintings of a quarry, dating from before their discovery.

This quarry was in use from the beginning to the middle of the last century and was still remembered by the older inhabitants of the district. The blast holes could still be seen when the cave was discovered. Luckily this did not collapse, but the blasts had given the rocks a severe shock and caused numerous cracks in the painted ceiling. The damage caused to the paintings was due to water seeping through these cracks. In 1925 Professor Obermaier consequently undertook systematic measures to protect them. He used cement to inject into the sinter cracks and waterproof the outside surface. The access to the cave was enlarged, the debris of rock on the floor of the cave removed, and massive protective walls erected.

In this way the temperature inside the cave was maintained at a steady level and the moisture content of the air kept between 96° and 97°. The temperature of the great hall, where the paintings were, was also regulated to remain between $13\frac{1}{2}$ and $14\frac{1}{2}$ degrees Centigrade throughout the year, i.e. to its original level, precision instruments being used in order to find the temperature which had proved so favourable for the preservation of the works.

The most important consideration was the moisture of the air; at more than 97° the paintings would have been destroyed, while in a drier atmosphere they would have disintegrated into a dusty soot.

Summary

The success of these measures has proved that to be preserved the paintings must be kept in a constantly damp condition and in this way their continued existence is now guaranteed.

This conclusion was also reached independently by us, although Obermaier's efforts were directed at the conservation of the paintings and our experiments at the discovery of the techniques used to paint them. We found that if the rock was kept damp, colours mixed only with water adhered well. Even though those colours not affected by sintering are still to a certain degree effaceable (also on the ceiling of Altamira), this at least proves that a binding medium was necessary neither for the application of the paint nor for their preservation. Moreover, organic media would almost certainly have perished very quickly.

That paintings have been preserved by moisture must surely be a unique phenomenon in art. Normally it is reputed to destroy them, especially if an organic medium has been used. In our own time great care is taken that the walls or rooms where a painting is to be executed are dry, even if they are exterior frescoes, and it is therefore only natural that a medium should be used, both to bind the colours and, more important, to ensure that the painting will remain dry. In the case of the prehistoric paintings of the Ice Age, the situation was reversed. These were painted on damp rock, almost invariably in unventilated caves, and they have lasted through being kept constantly damp.

We have therefore reached a conclusion directly opposite to all previous theories on the subject, namely, that in the paintings of the Ice Age, binding media were not used, or if they were, their significance was secondary. In fact their absence seems to be the very factor responsible for the preservation of these works. If they were used at all, it was only as a temporary vehicle for the paint, not as a means of conservation. In any case they were quickly destroyed and the pigments were preserved on the damp walls without their aid. To a certain extent these paintings seem to resemble frescoes, where the paint is also applied to a damp wall without a medium, and might be regarded as undried frescoes.

The painting procedure

The eastern Spanish paintings were executed, partly at least, in a glazing technique, or at any rate with very liquid paint. The figures are uniformly dark and flat. Although a few, such as those in the province of Teruel, are multi-coloured, most are in monochrome. The contours are white and merge into the interior of the paintings, which are a brownish colour. The method used in this particular case is actually not quite typical of the eastern Spanish glazing technique, for they show certain characteristics of the opaque works of Franco-Cantabria.

Very typical, on the other hand, are the recently discovered paintings in the Remigia cave in the Gasulla Gorge, near Ares del Maestre, in the province of Castellon. Here, in 1935, Obermaier found an unusual painting of ten warriors. The contours are roughly drawn in with pale, blackish paint and then filled in with light red. The lively effect of this monochrome painting is due to the tones below shining through the red paint, i.e. to the technique of glazing the colour. One of the warriors, who is lying down, is painted completely in black. His body is pierced with red and black arrows. This is one of the few eastern Spanish paintings in which there is more than one colour; the others are almost all painted exclusively in a beautiful monochrome ranging from brown-red to reddish-brown.

Another painting, which was accidentally discovered in 1907 at Cogul, and has in the meantime become almost invisible, is typical for the scenic representation of people and animals. It depicts women wearing skirts reaching almost to their knees, who appear to be dancing round a man. It is noteworthy that the colours are juxtaposed without transitions, in contrast to the Magdalenian paintings of Franco-Cantabria.

Women and animals: Cogul

As further typical examples may be mentioned the most important discoveries near Alpera, in the province of Albacete (1910). Here again we see a hunter with bow and arrow and the strange characteristic head-dress of feathers; there are also women, with skirts and head-dresses, men climbing ropes, and numerous animals of all kinds, mainly stags and prehistoric cattle.

The large frieze of Minateda, which was discovered in 1914, consists of hundreds of individual pictures, with single figures and animals which man hunted. This frieze was apparently worked on by several generations, since it contains extremely primitive paintings, more advanced ones on top of them, and on top of these, almost degenerate ones.

While making a scientific survey of the Remigia paintings Obermaier observed[55] that very liquid and transparent colours had been used here and that under certain circumstances these turned light red or violet on reddish or blue-grey rock. According to him the raw pigments (charcoal, manganese, hematite, and limonite) had been ground to powder and then prepared as a liquid. This could hardly have been done with water alone; probably fat, blood serum, or white of egg were used, with the slight possibility of plant juices. Apparently these paintings were executed entirely with liquid paint.

The technique used in eastern Spain is more complicated than the *al prima* method of the Franco-Cantabrians. The former were worked with very liquid colours. When the contours had been drawn in, they were filled in with a first, watery glaze, usually in grey (in this case probably with ink made from oak-apples).

It is at least technically possible that this process may have been reversed, and the possibility seems worth considering in view of the astonishing certainty of the contours, which are drawn with extremely fine lines, not more than a few millimetres wide. That it was easier to draw the contours accurately with the general form for guidance was proved by the reconstructions, about which more will be said below.

The third process was to cover the original glaze with a second and last layer, which was usually in a reddish colour. These layers do not always entirely coincide, either with each other or with the contours, which seems to suggest that there may be some truth in the theory that they were painted first (Obermaier). In any case it proves that the paint was applied in two layers. The technique of several superposed layers of colour gives the flat, unarticulated surfaces a certain amount of life.

The reconstructions

Some time ago Obermaier made reproductions of the eastern Spanish rock paintings *in situ*[55] and we could therefore make use of information provided by him. In our own reconstructions we used brushes made from reeds and tapering feathers. As in the reproductions of the Franco-Cantabrian paintings, the colours used were natural fragments of earth scraped and ground to a powder. In the originals the grey underpainting had probably been executed with paint made from manganese earth and diluted for transparency. For the next layer various tones of ochre were tried. The contours, which had to be only one thirty-second of an inch wide, were drawn with a very sharp, specially made brush; broad brushes were used for filling in the colour evenly. Since this technique was a fairly advanced and subtle one, it may be assumed that the tools had been made with some consideration for their purpose.

Stone was again used for the base to obtain a surface as close as possible to the originals. A very liquid paint could be obtained with a large variety of media, including blood, honey, and fish-oil, which were added to the unpurified earth colours. Fish-oil, however, cannot be seriously considered, in spite of the relative closeness of the sea. Other animal fats were out of the question, for the process of melting and keeping them warm would have been too complex for primitive man. It was also discovered that contrary to general belief, colours mixed with fat cannot be painted translucently on to rocks of the kind to be found in eastern Spain. Experiments were made with dry as well as damp rock, just as in the case of the Franco-Cantabrian techniques, because the niches under the overhangs, where most of the paintings are found, were not always damp, and the completely exposed rocks must have been even drier. The paintings on these latter which survive are also covered with a patina caused partly by sintering and partly by microflora, remains of microfauna and dust. Normally they are hardly visible; if they are sprayed with water they emerge quite clearly, vanishing again when they dry. The water creates the strange, deep light that we have already observed in *ganosis* and encaustic, and is also common to darkened oil paintings which are newly varnished, and to a certain extent to frescoes.[55]

Thus certain media were probably used for the glazing technique; this is evident from the layered execution alone. Fatty media have been excluded, and oil is unlikely owing to the difficulties involved in making a paint suitable for glazing without grinding the colours very fine. Lightly adhesive substances, on the other hand, such as blood diluted with water or honey dissolved in water, or perhaps even vegetable media, are very possible.

The original fragments and the question of conservation

As mentioned above, it was not possible to determine the use of organic binding vehicles by a chemical analysis of painted fragments of the original rock. On the other hand, the investigation of such original test-pieces yielded very definite results.[56] Since the fragments are very small, a coloured sketch with descriptive notes has been shown beside the original, which is enlarged three times.

The sintering process

When the oxygenous atmospheric water has penetrated the limestone formation long enough and has become saturated with calcium bicarbonate a reverse process begins. The water, saturated with calcium bicarbonate, evaporates, and calcium carbonate is detached in the form of a calcareous sinter. This evaporation takes place when water seeps

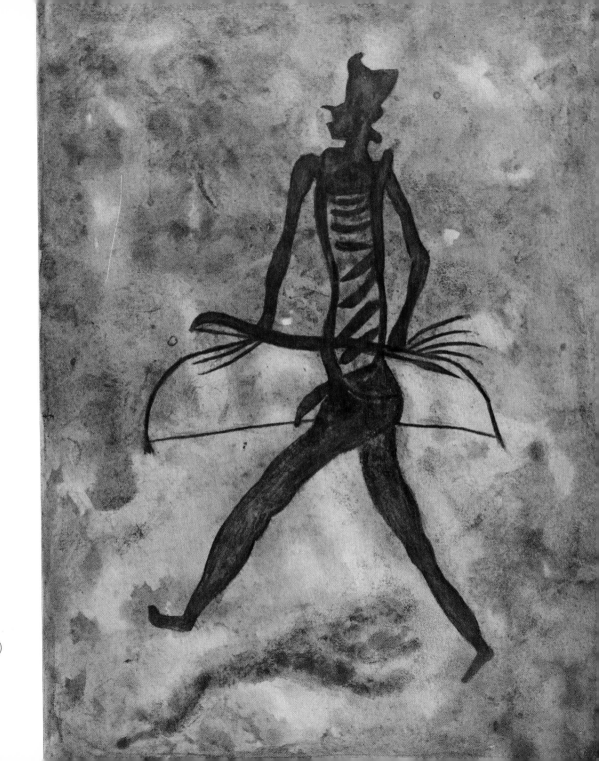

Striding archer:
Tormon (Teruel)

through the clefts in the rock into the caves and drops from the ceiling or runs down the walls. The deposits formed by this process make it geologically the opposite of the hollowing-out process. Climatically the latter phase was different from, and earlier than, the former.

Proof of the systematic nature of this process is that some of the paintings were found partly between two layers of such calcareous sinter; the upper layer had to be in part removed so that the paintings could be seen. If the paintings are completely covered they may be termed fossilized. When the rock is dry or the overhang is light, the sintering is not very marked, but even on the completely exposed paintings a veiled effect is to be observed.[57]

336

*Three technical reconstructions on rock,
using honey, blood, and fish-oil respectively
as binding media. By the author*

Summary

The technique used in the rock paintings of eastern Spain can be compared with a modern technique, which is also used on a hard, rock-like ground and leaves binding and conservation to a natural process. This is the fresco technique. In fresco the binding medium is the hydrate of lime in the plaster; in the prehistoric paintings it was the sinter-water, i.e. a solution of saturated bicarbonate. We make bold to call these 'natural frescoes'. Presumably the sintering was responsible for their preservation, so that the importance of binding media is small. It does not matter fundamentally whether the rock was damp or dry when the painting was executed, or whether the colours were mixed with aqueous media, vegetable juices, or blood. The moisture which seeped through the rocks, continuously or at intervals, eventually caused the sinter which created these natural frescoes. This was most easily formed if the pigment had been applied with little or no binding medium; in fact, strong media may have hindered the formation of sinter, at any rate in the early stages. The coating on the paintings on completely exposed rock faces proves that here moisture was also a contributory factor, though to a less marked degree.

Archer.
Valltorta cave

Fig. 1

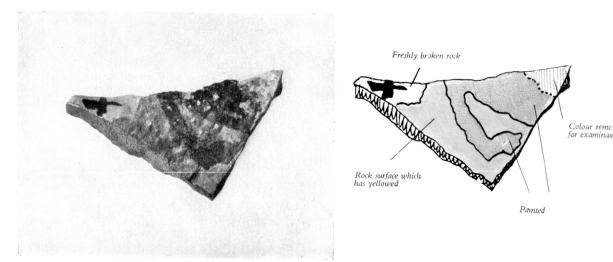

Freshly broken rock

Rock surface which
has yellowed

Colour remo
for examina

Painted

Fig. 1: On the left, the freshly broken stone; farther to the right, the normal rock surface, slightly yellow; beside it the actual painted surface in red. On the extreme right, a section from which the colour has been removed for investigation.

Fig. 2 shows, bottom, the freshly broken surface in light brown; on the right, the original yellowish surface, i.e. the actual crust. On the left, in brown, the painted area, with a piece removed from the centre for investigation. It may be seen that the red and brown colour rests immediately in the rough, warty, sintered limestone surface and appears to be completely amalgamated with it.

Fig. 3. The warty rock surface is still covered with well-preserved red colour; the small, light spots show where the surface crust and the colour have flaked off. This process may finally result in the painted surface rising and the layers of colour partially flaking off. The gradual decay of the paintings may be due to this unusual fossilization process. Noted also by Obermaier.

By contrast, the fact that the paintings have been preserved to the present day is largely due to the layers of sinter, up to several millimetres thick, which were created later by irrigation with mineral impregnated water. On some of the test-pieces it can be seen even with the naked eye that the colour is partly embedded between two layers of limestone, that is, between the rough, warty, original surface and the smooth, flat layers of the subsequently formed sinter.

Fig. 2

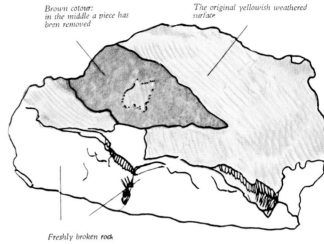

Brown colour:
in the middle a piece has
been removed

The original yellowish weathered
surface

Freshly broken rock

Fig. 3

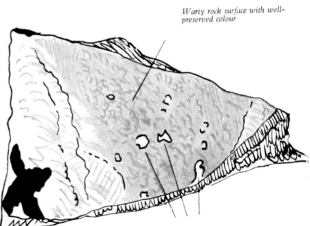

Warty rock surface with well-
preserved colour

The colouring has come off with the
surface of the stone

Fig. 4

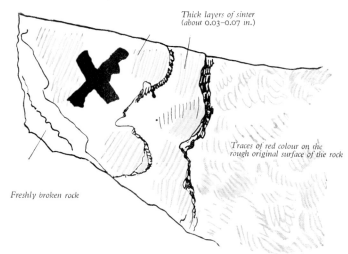

Thick layers of sinter
(about 0.03–0.07 in.)

Traces of red colour on the
rough original surface of the rock

Freshly broken rock

Figs. 4 and 5 show the remains of red colour on the original rough rock surface. Beside this can be seen the layers of sinter which cover it.

Fig. 6 shows this process in a similar way, except that here the red colour shows very clearly when a sinter crust is removed, beside the somewhat faded remains of colour on the exposed surface. This flaking off may of course proceed naturally and tends to do so under uneven stress.

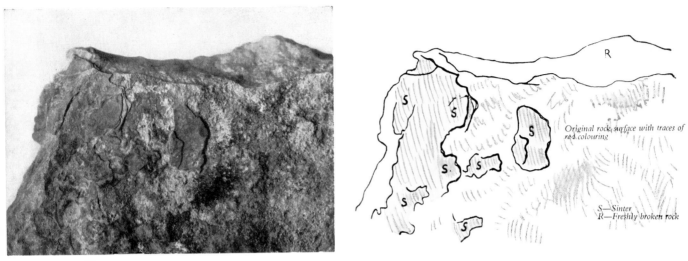

Fig. 5

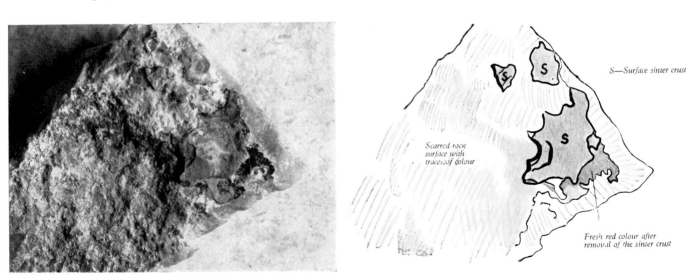

Fig. 6

REFERENCES

1 'The two opposite poles which are combined in the act of creating a work of art are the original conception and the medium. This conception, which is in some way stimulated in the artist's mind in a flash of inspiration or vision, is converted by the act of creation into plastic form, is physically realized through the medium of material substances, such as pigment, stone, wood, or sound, by subjecting itself progressively to the material in a series of physical processes. It becomes concrete, so to speak; it gives the material, by nature amorphous, the form of the spiritual concept, which by nature has no substance. The material, which originally bears no sort of relation to the world of the spirit, is overpowered by this process to such a degree that it assumes qualities originally quite foreign to it or comprehensible only through abstractions. In the finished work of art these qualities become concrete and visible. This ideal sense, made visible by material substances, is the basis for the effectiveness of every art form, and it far exceeds the comprehension of a purely rational viewpoint. The artist is the mediator between two polar elements, the idea and the material. He undertakes to bring about the transformation of an ideal conception into concreteness. This creative art, which begins in the world of the mind, penetrates further and further into the world of matter and ends in an irrevocable fusion of these two polar elements.' O. v. Pander.
2 Ernst Stockmeyer.
3 Erich Schwebsch.
4 Grosse.
5 Braque.
6 'A thorough knowledge of the medium is not enough. The artist must do more than merely experiment tentatively with the basic phenomena presented to him; the spirit of the material must approach the spirit of the man, who is disciplined by his vigilance.' v. Kügelgen.
7 Gottfried Semper: *Der Stil in den technischen und tektonischen Künsten*, 1860.
8 Kurt Herberts: *Aus der Maltechnik geboren.*

9 The paintings at Altamira are attributed to the middle Magdalenian Period, i.e. between 20,000 and 15,000 B.C.

10 The exception to this tendency was in eastern Russia and Siberia, where a more naturalistic form of art was practised.

11 See K. Herberts: *Untersuchungen über die Anwendbarkeit Historischer Malverfahren*.

12 K. Herberts: *Wände und Wandbild*.

13 See Georg Muche's fine book, *Buon Fresco*, which was written completely under its spell.

14 In Egypt and Crete, for instance.

15 If alterations are necessary they must be painted on in another technique, the so-called 'secco'.

16 An exception to this characteristic method are Mantegna's frescoes at Padua, painted in a very fine painstaking manner.

17 *Ueber die Technik der Griechischen Vasenmalerei*, which reverts to experiments made by Th. Schumann and Frau F. Oberlies.

18 1708–9; the inventor was Johann Friedrich Boettger.

19 e.g. by Camperdonck, Schlemmer, and Ida Kerkovius.

20 P. Meyer, *Byzantinische Mosaiken*, Bern, 1952.

21 *Die Japanische Malerei*, 1953.

22 After E. Diez: *Shan Shui*.

23 Grosse, *Die Ostasiatische Tuschmalerei*.

24 Ordinary watercolours may be redissolved indefinitely.

25 1266–1337.

26 H. Sachs, *Lehrbuch der Maltechnik*.

27 Cf. the chapter on 'Watercolour'.

28 Wehlte.

29 *Maltechnik für Kunstfreunde*.

30 710–95.

31 Introduction to Otto Kümmel, *Ostasiatisches Gerät*.

32 Many other materials are also used for the base, but wood is the most common.

33 *Il Libro dell' Arte, c.* 1400.

34 The lead stylus could not be used on coloured grounds, since the marks disappeared in the tone of the ground.

35 W. Ueberwasser: *Handzeichnungen europaeischer Meister des 14.–18. Jahrhunderts aus der Albertina*, Bern, 1948.

36 W. Schürmeyer.

37 *Meister des japanischen Farbholzschnittes*, Bern, 1947.

38 1592–1635.

39 Dürer had already been experimenting with dry-point, but it had then been forgotten again.

40 Translated by A. P. Laurie in *Greek and Roman Painting*, Cambridge University Press, 1910.

41 Vitruvius: *Ten Books on Architecture*, Book IV, Trans. M H. Morgan; Harvard, 1914.

42 Vitruvius: *Ten Books on Architecture*, Book IX, Trans. M. H. Morgan: Harvard, 1914.

43 *Technische Mitteilungen für Malerei*, Munich, 25 July 1937.

44 Director of Excavations at Pompeii and Herculaneum.

45 Published in the *Technische Mitteilungen für Malerei*, Nos. 10–12, 1940.

46 Trans. from the French of Didron. The bracketed phrases do not appear in Didron's Translation.

47 K. Herberts: *Anfänge der Malerei*.

48 *The Cave of Altamira*, 1937.

49 This theory is also put forward in Herbert's *10,000 Jahre Malerei und ihre Werkstoffe*.

50 See the illustration of an axe with a handle dating from the Neolithic Age on p. 325, which is in the author's collection.

51 L. Capitan, H. Breuil, D. Peyrony: *La Caverne de Font de Gaume aux Eyzies*, Monaco, 1910.

52 See extract quoted from *The Cave of Altamira*, p. 300.

53 See Frobenius: *Eritrea*.

54 See Penck and Brückner.

55 See *Quartär*, 1938.

56 Made possible by permission of Professor Obermaier through Herr Dr Stois of Munich. I should like to express my particular thanks to Professor Obermaier for the permission to publish these very rare test-pieces.

57 This is the process described more fully in the section dealing with the origin of caves.

LIST OF ILLUSTRATIONS

The Publishers would like to thank the following for permission to reproduce their works:

Alinari, Florence (41,101), Ursula Arndt, Düsseldorf (218), Bauverein für Arbeiterwohnungen, Darmstadt (52), Kupferstichkabinett, Berlin (185,189), F. Bruckmann-Verlag, Munich (99, 109, 145, 209), Kunstgutlager, Schloss Celle (59, 61, 63), Prof. Otto Coester, Düsseldorf (227), Cosmopress, Geneva, and Société de la Propriété Artistique des Dessins et Modèles, Paris (144-5), Willie Dirx, Wuppertal (88), Georg Dönges, Wuppertal (158), Hetjens-Museum, Düsseldorf (73), Felix Goll, Stuttgart (129), Iris-Verlag, Laupen bei Bern (115, 124), Willi Kannenberg, Schwelm (173, 174-6), Woldemar Klein Verlag, Baden-Baden (45), Kaiser-Wilhelm-Museum, Krefeld (125), Prof. Hans Kuhn, Berlin (107), Prof. Ferdinand Lammeyer, Frankfurt (139, 141, 143), Helmut Lander, Darmstadt (52), Prof. Georg Meistermann, Düsseldorf (80-85), Staatliche Graphische Sammlung, Munich (196), Fritz Niescher, Aachen (111), R. Piper & Co., Verlag, Munich (113), Hans Prähofer, Munich (53), Prestel-Verlag, Munich (132), Hans Jürgen Schlieker, Bochum (36), Kurt Schmidt, Stuttgart (150-1), Société de la Propriété Artistique des Dessins et Modèles, Paris (222), Dr. Franz Stoedtner, Institut für wissenschaftliche Projektion, Düsseldorf (191, 193, 213, 223), Südwestfunk, Baden-Baden (107), Bayer, Versicherungskammer, Munich (53), Wallraf-Richartz-Museum, Cologne (147), Prof. Kurt Wehlte, Stuttgart (103, 105-6), Prof. Hans Wentzel, Stuttgart (77), Dr. Paul Wolff & Tritschler, Lichtbildwerkstätten, Frankfurt (37), Landesbildstelle Württemberg, Stuttgart (77), Kunst- und Museumsverein Wuppertal (133), Städtliche Museum Wuppertal (154-5, 197, 211, 215, 217, 229-32).